Financing and Building an E-Commerce Venture

MARC KRAMER

Prentice
Hall Press

Library of Congress Cataloging-in-Publication Data

Kramer, Marc.
    Financing and building an e-commerce venture / Marc Kramer.
        p.   cm.
    Includes index.
    ISBN 0-7352-0198-6
    1. Electronic commerce.   2. Venture capital.   I. Title.

HF5548.32 .K73 2001
658.8' 4—dc21   2001018544

Acquisitions Editor: *Luis Gonzalez*
Production Editor: *Sharon L. Gonzalez*
Formatting/Interior Design: *Robyn Beckerman*

Printed in the United States of America

10 9 8 7 6 5 4 3 2 1

ISBN 0-7352-0198-6

 **Prentice Hall Press** Paramus, NJ 07652

http://www.phdirect.com

DEDICATION

I want to thank my wife, Jackie, and my daughters, Ariel and Sydney, for being so supportive and understanding as this book took up many weekends and parts of vacations to write.

I appreciate the editing efforts of Gail Jones. I want to thank Fred Lipman, a partner at Blank Rome Cominsky and McCauley, for providing various sample legal documents; Dr. Jeffrey Sohl, executive director of the University of New Hampshire Center for Venture Research; and all of the professionals who allowed me to interview them for this book.

I want to thank Prentice Hall and especially my editor, Luis Gonzalez, and his staff for their support and encouragement and for allowing me to write this book, and my agent, Sheree Bykofsky, for introducing me to Prentice Hall.

Finally, I want to acknowledge an Internet visionary, entrepreneur, client, and friend, Abigail Cohen, founder and president/CEO of TheArtBiz.com, who unfortunately passed away at the age of 27. I hope this book will spur other Abigail Cohens to turn their dreams into reality.

CONTENTS

PREFACE

In the mid-1990s, Jeff Bezos packed up his family and moved to Seattle, Washington, and launched Amazon. As Bezos was launching Amazon on the West Coast, Jason and Matt Olim were starting CDNow on the East Coast—and so began the Internet gold rush. Thousands of entrepreneurs on college campuses and at Fortune 1000 companies left their educational pursuits and steady jobs for a chance to change the world and become the next Rockefeller or Gates.

The rush started with entrepreneurs offering shoppers the ability to buy whatever they wanted whenever they wanted at a price they deemed acceptable. Then came people like Walter Buckley III (a former Safeguard Scientifics vice president), who with another Safeguard board member's son, Ken Fox, foresaw a future where business-to-business (B2B) markets could be aggregated and controlled through the use of technology. They created online marketplaces to sell everything from cattle to electricity to parts for wastewater plants through their publicly traded venture capital company, Internet Capital Group.

Within months of Buckley and Fox touting their vision, their patriarch, Warren "Pete" Musser (chairman of Safeguard Scientifics), talked about selling the infrastructure and tools needed for companies such as Internet Capital Group to be a success.

As I am writing this book, the gods of Wall Street have turned their backs on online retail because so many of these companies are not profitable, and Wall Street has questions about how many online markets can succeed and how pre-Internet companies, such as Ford and General Electric, will fit in.

In the 1980s the most active venture funds were seeing 25 to 100 business plans a week. The only people who were looking for funding were those who didn't fit into corporate America who had patentable ideas that they believed could change the world. Today, venture funds such as Flatiron Partners and New Enterprise Associates need their own post offices, as they are flooded with 500 to 1,000 business plans a week.

Even my 10-year-old daughter, Ariel, spoke to me about an idea she had and asked me to help her with a business plan to find funding for the idea. Every day I read a newsletter called *Venture Wire (www.venturewire.com),* which typically averages 21 letter-size pages describing companies that have been blessed by the lords of venture capital to be worthy of receiving capital. What are the odds of receiving professional money? Companies such as Safeguard Scientifics and Internet Capital Group review over 52,000 business plans a year though they each fund only 25 to 30. My calculator can't account for that many zeros to the right of the decimal point to determine the odds.

The hardest part of starting any venture isn't developing or getting someone to buy your product or service, it's finding someone to invest in it. Surprisingly, every publication that interviews venture capitalists hears the same refrain, "There is too much money chasing too few good deals." I can tell you that I haven't met the entrepreneur yet who would agree with that statement as they are launching their new enterprise. Once the first million is put in, the next million is a lot easier to come by.

Regardless of the odds of raising capital, I am a firm believer that any person starting an enterprise will provide his family with a better chance of stability and long-term financial security than he could by working for any company in the Fortune 1000. I wrote this book because I work with entrepreneurs every day of the week and I couldn't find a book that walked the entrepreneur through what is needed to build a company that can attract investors and build great wealth.

There are books on how to write a business plan, how to build a successful management team, how to build a good board of directors, and how to raise venture capital. Unfortunately, until now no book has brought all of them together. This book walks you through the following:

- Selecting the right opportunities
- Developing a business plan that attracts the attention of venture capitalists
- Presenting your business when meeting venture capitalists
- Addressing the types of questions a venture capitalist will ask
- Developing operating and sales/marketing plans that help you obtain venture capital

- Choosing the employees who will make your dream a reality
- Selecting the advisors and board members that will help you grow your company
- Identifying the right venture capitalists
- Negotiating with the venture capitalists so you keep enough of the company to make all of your hard work worthwhile

What is the secret to attracting venture capital and building a successful company? The answer is simple, but the process is arduous and one that only those with the convictions of revolutionaries willing to die for their cause will follow. To succeed, all of the following have to be perfectly aligned:

- The founder has to be brilliant or good at attracting brilliant people.
- The founder can't be a micromanager.
- The concept has to solve a problem and alleviate a pain.
- The founder has to get very lucky and meet the one person or group who gets excited about her idea.
- The founder or someone on his team has to be very good at raising money.
- The company has to be very good at building visibility and creating an aura of invincibility.

If you follow the steps in this book and think about what the entrepreneurs and venture capitalists have to say, then you will enhance your chances of raising capital and someday you may obtain the ultimate dream of every entrepreneur—to take your company public or be bought by a company that is already public or is going public.

First, you must read this book and then you must defy the odds of raising capital. If you have the strength of your convictions and buyers are willing to write a check for your product or service, you will probably succeed.

Wall Street and venture capitalist reaction to anything over a short period of time is always excessive whether that reaction is elation or castigation. Over the long run, investors appreciate and reward entrepreneurs and businesses that provide their customers with a way to enhance revenue or reduce cost, or both. If you listen to your customer, hire the best people, and write out your road map, you will be one of the winners, and no stock market downturn will stop you.

1

STEPS FOR IDENTIFYING GOOD
ONLINE BUSINESS OPPORTUNITIES

Over 1 million companies are selling products over the Internet, according to The Gartner Group, one of the leading Internet market research companies. Possibly by the time you read this book, it will be in the tens of millions.

The Internet is just in its infant stages regardless of how the stock market treats it. Only half of the homes in the United States and less than 10% of the rest of the world on average, according to Cyber Atlas, are online. For the retail sector, that means there are still plenty of people who haven't developed any allegiances to a particular site, and (aside from Amazon and E-trade) there are few universal brand names.

In the business-to-business market the traditional brand names such as DuPont, Ford, and General Electric are starting to map out and implement online strategies. Every day another business exchange is popping up. Some companies, such as Vertical Net, have developed more than 50 business exchanges. At this writing, there are business exchanges for the following:

- Auto parts
- Business supplies
- Chemicals
- Commercial construction
- Commercial property management supplies

1

- Electricity market
- Hospital supplies
- Printing
- Residential construction
- School supplies
- Steel
- Used parts
- Water

If you are thinking of starting some type of e-commerce company and are afraid that all of the opportunities have been taken, you're wrong. Many types of opportunities are available now. They may not be initial public offering (IPO) ventures, but they may be of interest to existing public companies or companies that are looking to roll up similarly focused companies into one national company. This is typically called a rollup in the investment banking world.

REGIONAL CONSUMER

There are a variety of opportunities in the regional consumer space that aren't dominated by a name brand player such as Amazon or Yahoo!.

- *Automotive.* Companies that allow car shoppers to find the car they want online and put together a loan package before consummating the purchase of the car can be valuable time-savers and serve as a way for local dealers to keep regional customers happy.

- *Gifts.* Companies that list gifts by product type and then allow consumers to type in the gift they are looking for, purchase it online, and have the option to pick up or have the product delivered will provide a lot of value. Townspeople can support local stores and save time by not having to get in their cars and go from store to store trying to find what they need.

- *Handyman.* Companies that provide online access to screened contractors to do work ranging from paneling walls and painting to landscaping are valued by two-income families or families with a spouse who travels a lot for work.

• *Restaurants.* Companies that can present a list of local sit-down and take-out restaurants will allow local people to make reservations and delivery orders online.

REGIONAL BUSINESS

Although we are a global economy, 80% of business transactions, according to the Small Business Administration, take place locally. There are numerous local B2B opportunities.

• *Business supplies.* Small independent business supply stores can provide their customers with an easy way to order and have supplies delivered to their businesses without anyone having to take time to shop.

• *Catering.* Companies are looking for internal and external catering. A site that provides information on sizes, costs, and availability of facilities can charge the provider a fee when users contract online for catering services.

• *Construction.* Regional construction firms are always scrambling to find skilled labor. A company that provides a database outlining the skills of individual workers and their availability will provide tremendous value to local contractors.

• *Movers.* Companies typically go to the Yellow Pages to find someone to move them. A website that allows users to fill out the number of rooms they need to move and then provides quotes and available dates from regional moving firms is now beginning to take off.

• *Professional services.* Companies that allow business leaders to type in the service they are looking for and then to find the companies that offer it and their prices can create opportunities for local providers. They can also reduce time buyers need to find qualified help and can provide competitive pricing.

INTERNATIONAL BUSINESS

Companies outside the United States are beginning to catch up with companies in the United States in terms of the types of products and services offered to both consumers and businesses. Many U.S. companies have extended their brands to Europe (Yahoo!, for example) or are partnering with European and Asian companies, as Internet Capital Group is doing. There are still many opportunities in the consumer and business-to-business markets:

- *Boarding schools.* Professionals who are transferred abroad and have children would like to be able to go to a website that provides a list, pictorial description, comments, and the capability to find more information and apply online.

- *Corporate partners.* Companies in the United States and abroad are looking for corporate partners to extend their reach. A site that provides names, contact information, and descriptions of companies that are looking for partners to distribute products and services would be very valuable.

- *Financing.* Few of us know the names of banks outside of our own country. A site that allows companies to obtain financing on an international basis would be a strong attraction to all sizes of companies, especially middle-market companies that aren't prime targets for large money center banks.

- *Professional services.* A site that provides contact information by country on technology consulting, legal, accounting, and other professional services would provide companies moving to an area with easy access to needed professional support and provide new business opportunities.

IDENTIFYING MARKETS THAT AREN'T SATURATED

Before worrying about how much money you want to raise and who will compose your management team, you need to identify the market in which you want to do business. Regardless of how good a team you put together and how successful you have been in the past, tackling a market that has a lot of players or a few very large and well-funded ones is a fight you want to avoid. It's also a brawl that investors shy away from because the blood spilled will make it difficult or impossible to build a sustainable and profitable business.

When entrepreneurs come to us with an idea, we ask them to check the following sources to get a sense of how crowded the market they want to enter is:

- *Search engines.* Go to each of the major search engines (*www.yahoo.com*, *www.altavista.com*, *www.excite.com*, *www.lycos.com*, and *www.infoseek.com*) and type in the name of the industry you want to focus on. Check out the first 20 to 30 websites. If the number of companies popping up is small, then type in a variety of names that best describe what you would like to do. This is a first-level screen.

- *Trade associations.* Contact the Association of Association Executive Directors (*www.asae.org*) and ask if it knows of a trade association in the area you are interested in. There are trade associations for everything you can think of. Ask for the head of research or the sales department and describe the business you are interested in and ask him if he knows of anyone in that business. You don't have to tell him you plan to start a company in that area.

- *Research firms.* Contact the major research firms such as The Gartner Group (*www.gartner.com*), Forester Research (*www.forester.com*), and USADATA (*www.usadata.com*) and speak to the analysts and researchers who cover the field.

- *Brokerage houses.* Contact the research departments of brokerage houses such as Merrill Lynch (*www.merrill.com*) and Morgan Stanley *www.morganstanley.com*).

- *Venture capital sites.* Go to the National Venture Capitalist Association (*www.nvca.org*), which has links to all of its members. A great newsletter to subscribe to is Venture wire (*www.technologicpartners.com*), which is put out by Technology Partners, a venture capital publication company. V-capital, an online investment bank, developed a destination site (*www.v-capital.com/vcdirectory.htm*) to find venture capital and service providers who work with venture-capital–backed companies. *www. vfinance.com* provides names of venture capital funds by areas of interest.

- *Venture capital funds.* Type in the words *venture capital* on Yahoo! and you will find a list of venture capitalists in alphabetical order. Most venture capitalists are afraid to fund business concepts that have been funded by many of the name funds such as Safeguard Scientifics (*www.safeguard.com*), New Enterprise Associates (*www.nea.com*), Internet Capital Group (*www.internetcapital.com*), Flatiron Partners (*www.flatironpartners.com*), and Kleiner Perkins Caufield & Byers (*www.kpcb.com*) because they are concerned that the field is too crowded.

- *Publications.* Three excellent publications can tell you the hot areas in Internet commerce, who the players are in those areas, and who is funding them: *The Industry Standard* (*www.thestandard.com*), *Business 2.0* (*www.business2.com*), and *Interactive Week* (*www.interactive-week.com*).

Once you have done a thorough search of potential competition and have satisfied yourself that you have something unique that people are willing to pay for, you need to begin mapping out a success strategy.

TEN OBSTACLES TO BUILDING A SUCCESSFUL E-COMMERCE COMPANY

The following 10 obstacles must be overcome in order to build a successful e-commerce company:

1. *Gorillas.* The Internet, as a business opportunity, is still early in its life cycle. The competition for new markets has accelerated. As previously noted, there are still many good opportunities. The business concepts that have the greatest chances of getting funded are ones where the large companies haven't developed an Internet presence, which provides the entrepreneur with a chance to build the model and invite the gorillas to become partners.

2. *Mediocre team.* Don't settle for mediocrity when putting together your management team. Go after the best possible people and don't worry about whether you can afford to pay them. One of my former clients started an online company for the institutional investment field. He needed an industry giant to join his team. The man he wanted was mak-

ing $5 million a year. When my former client told the venture capitalist (VC) what the person was making, the VC told my former client to sell the giant on the potential upside of the stock and the challenge of building a successful venture. My former client not only got his man, but the giant agreed to take no salary in lieu of 5% of the company's stock. This individual's willingness to join my former client was highlighted on CNBC and CNNFN and in all the major industry magazines, which encouraged other star players to leave high-paying positions and join him. By attracting marquee talent, my former client was able to raise over $20 million.

3. *Inexperienced web developers.* A few years ago, anyone who developed more than one website was considered experienced. Today, an experienced developer has created at least 50 to 100 websites and 25% of those sites should have some form of significant interactivity associated with them such as e-commerce, video and audio streaming, and password-protected databases. Web developers charge anywhere from $80 to $200 an hour. The key to selecting a developer is finding one who can successfully develop a technology-proficient website that is scalable and easy to manage internally. Just as important, you want a developer who understands the market you are going into so you don't have to explain industry nuances to her. I had a client in the medical field who was developing a password-protected website for doctors. I introduced him to three developers, one of whom had significant experience working with pharmaceutical companies. The other two were great developers, but it would have taken the client a good month and a lot of money to explain to them what the one developer already knew about doctors.

4. *Unimpressive advisory board.* Investors and employees are always interested in who is on the company's advisory board. Quality advisory board members give business concepts and the entrepreneurs running them a certain "Good Housekeeping" seal of approval. Investors also place significant value on advisors who have the ability to open doors and create sales opportunities or to recruit experienced employees and investors.

5. *Inappropriate consultants.* Picking the right attorneys, accountants, website developers, and other business consultants is important because if the consultants have strong reputations and have dealt with the venture capitalists that are looking at your business concept, there is a

greater chance of attracting funding. Using established professional service providers says a lot about the entrepreneur and the concept. In Philadelphia, where I reside, there are certain accountants and lawyers who significantly enhance a company's chances of obtaining capital just because they agreed to work with the company.

6. *Lack of publicity.* Getting publicity is very hard because there are so many Internet companies and the Internet is no longer a curiosity. The reason someone would write a check to invest is the same reason the press would write a story—because you have something different to offer. Hire a good public relations firm with strong connections. We hired a public relations firm in Boston called Newman Communications and in one day it had me on CNNFN, Bloomberg Television, and Voice of America and arranged a meeting with a reporter from *Forbes.* The number of new visitors and sales rose dramatically.

7. *Poor marketing.* Hiring a good public relations firm is important, but having experienced marketing professionals who understand how to get to your target market is more crucial. A friend of mine has a website, *www.investorforce.com,* that markets to institutional money managers. His marketing team is made up of top marketing professionals from the best-known names in his industry. They know what end users like to read, how they think, and what they like and don't like.

8. *Unaggressive sales.* Marketing can be compared to the Navy during the D-Day invasion in that it can let everyone know you are coming by firing artillery such as direct marketing pieces, print advertising, and sponsorships. Sales can be compared to the Marines who hit the beaches and needed to secure the real estate. An experienced, aggressive sales team with a strong database of past customers will shorten the sales cycle and allow your cash to stretch further.

9. *Inexperienced financial leader.* Don't hire a glorified bookkeeper. Hire an experienced chief financial officer who knows how to reduce costs without inhibiting marketing and sales from doing their jobs. A good CFO also knows how to speak to and sell investors on your concept. A good CFO has strong bank, investment bank, and venture capital contacts. As president of the business, you don't want to be the only one focused on raising capital.

10. *No strategic partners.* Because of the high cost of building brand awareness in the e-commerce or Internet product area, the companies that don't have quality strategic partners will ultimately fail because they won't have enough capital to acquire enough companies to become profitable. This is extremely important when the Initial Public Offering (IPO) market is closed. One of my clients, Ecom-Energy *(www.ecomenergy.com)* sells energy to health care facilities. It has developed a partnership with a worldwide leader in health care consulting that is going to bring it 3,000 corporate buyers. If the client had to do that on its own, even with an experienced team, it would take two or three years to build that type of critical mass.

CHAPTER SUMMARY

Before you commit yourself to a particular dot.com concept—whether as entrepreneur, employee, or investor—make sure you have thoroughly researched the marketplace. Once you have done that, make sure you have recruited the best possible team. No industry that I know of has been a stronger magnet for top talent than the Internet because of its newness, intellectual stimulation, and promise of riches. Because of that strong attraction, the competition for eyeballs and product sales will be intense. If you believe your concept is unique and your team strong and aggressive, then be prepared for 10-to-14–hour days, six to seven days a week.

Not every opportunity has to be one that dominates a market or has the potential to go public in order to attract funding. The concept does have to have the potential to be acquired or to create strong enough cash flow to make the investors liquid.

2

WRITING A
BUSINESS PLAN

This past summer while watching my nine-year-old play lacrosse, I overheard two other parents talking about ideas they had for a new Internet startup. You could see the dollar signs in their eyes and you could tell they were thinking about the millions and possibly billions they were going to make once they got started.

One of the men said, "Let's just build a website and raise some cash." The other guy asked if they needed some type of plan. The one with big dreams said the concept and the site itself would be enough.

Shacks are built without plans. Strong, enduring homes with few problems are developed using architectural plans, because selecting the wrong layout, building site, or materials could result in a house that falls in on top of you. Similarly, a business plan is the architectural blueprint for your business.

A business plan should be a realistic view of the expectations and long-term objectives for a business. It provides the framework within which the company must operate and, ultimately, succeed or fail. For managers or entrepreneurs seeking external support, the plan is the most important sales document that they are ever likely to produce as it is key to focusing the company and to raising capital. Preparation of a comprehensive plan will not guarantee success in raising funds or mobilizing support, but lack of a sound plan will almost certainly ensure failure.

A formal business plan serves the following critical functions:

- It helps managers or entrepreneurs to clarify, focus, and research the development and prospects of the business or project.
- It provides a well-thought-out, logical framework within which a business can develop and pursue business strategies over the next three to five years.
- It serves as a basis for discussion with potential investors.
- It offers a benchmark against which actual performance can be measured and reviewed.

The length of a business plan, including financial projections, should be 25 to 35 single-spaced pages on average. A business plan typically includes the following sections:

- *Executive summary* (three to four pages). This is the most important section of your business plan. Venture capital companies such as Internet Capital Group and Flatiron Partners receive 10,000 to 24,000 business plans a year. Your executive summary has to grab the readers' attention or it will be cast aside and they will go on to the next plan. The executive summary is a condensed version of the business plan. The executive summary should have the following subheadings:

  Problem/opportunity. The first question every venture capitalist asks is "What problem are you solving?" Companies use an Internet site to reduce their costs of doing business, to find new sales leads, or to obtain hard-to-find information.

  Solution. Here you describe what your company has to offer to solve the problem you just outlined.

  Market. A paragraph or two describe the size of the marketplace.

  Marketing of company. Briefly discuss to whom the company will be marketed and list tactics the company plans to use to build brand awareness.

  Revenue streams. Describe how your company makes money.

Competition. Describe the competition in one or two paragraphs.

Competitive advantage. In a bulleted list, give reasons why your business model is better than the competition's.

Management. Describe each executive in one or two sentences.

Capital requirements. State the amount of money you are looking to raise and what you plan to do with it.

- *Description of the business* (one page). For an e-commerce company, this description should include the market the business is going after and the end user who decides whether to buy from the site. For example, I am on the board of a company called rfpMarket.com. The description for this business would be as follows:

> rfpMarket.com provides business and publication portal and destination sites with the ability to offer their users an online conduit to find a variety of independent business contractors in marketing, technology, and management. rfpMarket.com private labels its service so that users think the site they are using is providing the service.

- *Company objectives* (one page). The company should have short-term objectives that cover years 1 and 2 and long-term objectives that start at year 3 and end at year 5. The objectives should be quantifiable and focus on the following:

  - Target for number of new customers
  - Target for number of retained customers
  - Expected year company will be cash-flow–positive
  - Anticipated revenue for first two years
  - Anticipated revenue by year 5

- *Market for the business* (two to three pages). Like an attorney making her case in front of a jury, the company has to make its case using industry sources and facts to support its supposition about why its product/service is needed. A great source to find marketing information is *www.cyberatlas.com*. This website contains research from all of the top market research firms.

- *Sales* (one to two pages). Describe in detail to whom the company is targeting its product and what tactics will be used to sell the product. For example, the targeted user might be a company president and the tactics to be used might be direct mail, trade shows, and seminars.

- *Marketing strategy* (one to two pages). Describe in detail how the company plans to develop a recognizable name through the use of various marketing tools such as direct mail, print advertising, and banner advertising.

- *Revenue* (one to two pages). Describe each source of revenue.

- *Retention plan* (one to two pages). The hardest part of building a business is trying to retain your customers. Too many entrepreneurs focus on the initial sale and not on how they plan to support new customers once they have committed. Getting new customers is a lot more difficult and financially costly than retaining existing customers, especially in the dot.com world. Amazon reported in the first quarter of 2000 that 80% of its orders are coming from past buyers. This is a great sign that the company will have a future, not just a past.

- *Competition* (three to five pages). The worst mistake entrepreneurs can make in developing their business plan is to say that they don't have any competition. Everyone has competition, whether it is direct or indirect. You need to perform a strengths-and-weaknesses analysis on each competitor. I typically paste the competition's home page on top of the analysis. Also, a chart showing the differences between your company and the competition will strengthen your case for funding.

- *Management* (two to three pages). Include a one-paragraph description of the backgrounds and duties of each member of the management team. If you have board members, a one-paragraph biography of each person is appropriate.

- *Professional advisors* (one to two pages). List your professional advisors such as lawyer, accountant, marketing consultant, public relations firm, executive recruiting firm, sales consultant, and business plan developer. If an investor sees a name he knows and respects, he's more likely to be interested in the business.

• *Operations plan* (one to two pages). In one to two paragraphs discuss how each section of the business will operate. Cover administration, technology, web development, and accounting.

• *Launch plan* (two to three pages). Here a spreadsheet details what you plan to do in each of the company's first 12 months of existence. This covers the number of new customers signed, the number of new employees by position, when outside vendors will be hired, what they will be employed to do, and so on.

• *Financials* (three to five pages). Here give a one-year cash flow statement and five-year financial projections. You don't need an accountant to do this for you. If you know how to operate an Excel spreadsheet, you can do it yourself. Accountants would be a waste of money at this point because they would rely on you to tell them your revenue forecasts and to list and explain each of your expense categories. Notes detailing the calculations you used to build your forecasts should appear at the end of the financials. Have an accountant review the financials to make sure all of the formulas are accurate. Nothing is more embarrassing than numbers that don't add up correctly.

Just as no two businesses are alike, neither are business plans. Nonetheless, most plans follow a tried and tested structure, so general advice on preparing a plan is universally applicable. The following suggestions will help you create a quality plan:

1. The most important and difficult sections to prepare relate to marketing and sales, as these can make or break not only the business plan but also the business itself!

2. When putting together financial projections, create a five-year forecast and a one-year cash flow statement. Microsoft Office comes with financial spreadsheets and financial modeling options. Two other good software packages designed to assist with business plan writing are Plan A (from Internet Capital Bulletin Board, Inc.) and Plan Write (from Business Resource Software, Inc.). Both packages ask the user a series of questions. When the user finishes answering all of the questions, a formal business plan with financials is provided.

3.   When drafting the plan, be positive but realistic about the business's prospects, and explicitly recognize and respond honestly to shortcomings and risks.

4.   The management section of the plan is crucial. It should demonstrate the management's experience, balance, ability, and commitment. Remember that the fate of the company is not in the product but in the management team.

5.   Avoid unnecessary jargon, economize on words, and use short, crisp sentences and bullet points. Always make sure that all words are spelled correctly. When there are significant issues, break the text into numbered paragraphs or sections, and relegate detail to appendices.

6.   Get a qualified outsider to review your plan in draft form. Be prepared to adjust the plan in the light of the reviewer's comments.

7.   Support market and sales projections with market research. Ensure that there is a direct relationship between market analysis, sales forecasts, and financial projections. Realistically assess competitors' positions and possible responses.

8.   Restrict the level of detail on product specifications and technical issues.

9.   Be realistic about sales expectations, profit margins, and funding requirements. Ensure that financial ratios are in line with industry norms. Do not underestimate the cost and time required for product development, market entry, securing external support, or raising capital. Consider the possibility of the halve-double rule: Halve the sales projections and double the cost and time required.

10.   When looking for external equity, be realistic about the value of the business, risks involved, and possible returns, and be sure to indicate possible exit mechanisms. Put yourself in the shoes of an investor and remember the golden rule: He who has the gold makes all the rules.

If those parents at my daughter's game hope to be successful, they had better have a plan or else those visions of lying out on beach chairs on St. Martin will have no chance of becoming a reality.

HOW IMPORTANT IS A BUSINESS PLAN TO A VENTURE CAPITALIST?

Glenn T. Rieger is president of Cross Atlantic Capital Partners, Inc., and a managing director of Cross Atlantic Technology Fund and The Co-Investment 2000 Fund, L.P. These two funds have $270 million of committed capital. Prior to April 1999, Glenn was senior vice president in charge of business development for Safeguard Scientifics (NYSE: SFE). In this position, he developed and oversaw merger, acquisition, and investment opportunities for Safeguard. In addition, he served as a business partner and director for five of Safeguard's partnership companies and was materially responsible for such successful investments as US Interactive Inc. (NASDAQ: USIT) and Pac-West Telecommunications (NASDAQ: PACW). Glenn is a graduate of Colby College and has an MBA from the Wharton School of the University of Pennsylvania.

How important is the vision of the CEO/entrepreneur?

I think the vision is very important, but it isn't the most important element. The most important thing is the market opportunity. The CEO has to have a vision for a market opportunity that is big and growing.

How important is a business plan?

It is an important road map and it can take lots of twists and turns. Things will be added and subtracted.

What is the proper length of a plan?

I think you can get the whole message across in 20 to 25 pages. You have to have a punchy first page or two. You have to get across that there is a big market opportunity. You have to convey you have the right team to execute the plan.

How short can it be without substituting content?

I have seen very good business plans that are 10 pages long. It's a matter of getting your idea through concisely. If a VC begins to engage on the plan, he/she will undoubtedly ask for more details.

How important is grammar?

We don't study the grammar of the plan. If there are lots of errors, you might wonder about the intellect of the writer, but we really don't focus on that.

To what degree do investors expect new ventures to meet expectations, financial predictions, and task deadlines?

The one certainty in this business is that whatever is stated in the plan is not what will happen. We study the plan and try to gather information concerning whether there is enough opportunity, especially if the market shifts on them. We don't apply a discount factor. Only two out of 10 entrepreneurs will hit what they project.

How important is a barrier to entry?

If you are doing a pure enabling technology and there are patents and trademarks involved, then it is important. If you are a professional services company like Cambridge Technology, there is little that is protectable. Your IP [Internet provider] walks out the door every night and it's all about first-mover advantage. In the Internet there are few barriers to entry. First-mover advantage is important.

One of the risks in business-to-consumer businesses on the Internet is that it is hard to maintain the first-mover advantage. In business-to-business you can have a superior technology or have a special niche and it's a matter of being the best over time and not necessarily being first.

Do VCs put any weight on the exit strategy?

We talk about the exit strategy when making an investment decision. We talk about the likelihood of an IPO or strategic sale. It needs to be put in the plan because every VC wants to know how they are going to get their investment out.

Do you read every business plan front to back?

No! There aren't enough hours in the day.

Which sections do you read that determine whether you are going to read the rest of the plan?

I read the executive summary, the management team, market description, and competitive position. I believe the competitive positioning should have its own section. If the executive summary grabs me, then I will continue to read. If I get through the whole plan, then they probably will be invited to meet with us.

How important is presentation (such as using graphics and color) in a business plan?
It's not that important. It doesn't do anything for me.

What parts of the business plan do you find typically weak?
The marketing and competitive positioning. I can't tell you how many times we read about some analyst reports that say B2B will be a trillion-dollar market and I say, "So what part of it are you going after and how big is that market?" They also will say they have no competition. But there is always competition, whether it is direct or indirect. The financials are problematic. Who knows what financials will look like three to five years out.

What do you look for when reading the financials?
How much cash is needed today, what is the burn rate and what they will do when they run out, what are the staffing requirements, and can they operate on a profitable basis. We can't afford to fund businesses that can't tell us when they will stop losing money. I have seen hundreds of plans that don't show any profit for the first five years.

CHAPTER SUMMARY

Developing a business plan is absolutely essential regardless of whether or not you are trying to raise money. You need a business plan to see what flaws your business model may have and to communicate a clear vision and direction for your employees, board members, and potential investors. Appendix A presents a sample business plan for a fictitious electronic commerce company called Worldfunding.com.

3

WRITING
OPERATING AND LAUNCH PLANS

Writing a business plan will help you sell the concept to an investor. The next document an investor will ask for is an operating plan. The operating plan will provide a greater level of detail than the business plan on how you plan to manage the business. It will show the investor that you have given it some thought and have some understanding of what it will take to build the business.

When writing the operating plan, you will find that some of your assumptions in your business plan either are wrong or will take longer to put in place than you put in your business plan, or you will need to add positions that you hadn't previously considered. For example, I wrote a business plan for an e-commerce business that assists companies in obtaining financing. One of the positions that we had not planned for (and none of the investors had asked about) was a person to interface with the banks that would be providing our users with financing. We needed to create a vice president's position and then provide funding for support staff.

ELEMENTS OF AN OPERATING PLAN

Whatever operating plan you write in the beginning of the company's life is sure to evolve and change within the first year of operation. Few companies that aren't looking for funding ever write an operating plan, but it is a discipline that will improve the company's overall chances of growing and being successful. Every investor will be interested in the following 10 basic parts to an e-commerce operating plan:

1. *Website development.* E-commerce companies usually develop a prototype website to show investors. What investors want to see is the plan for the next generation of the website, what it will cost to fund the next phase, and how long it will take to build. Many of today's investors in e-commerce businesses have experience at developing e-commerce sites, so when they look at the plan they can make suggestions and may have ideas on who would be best to implement the plan. At this stage of the company's life, outside of selecting the right managers to guide the business, this is the most critical part of the business and one of the biggest cost centers.

2. *Office rollout strategy.* If you are developing a business-to-business e-commerce business, you can't rely solely on marketing and public relations to drive sales to your website. You will need to hire salespeople who will visit prospective customers, demonstrate the website, and get targeted users to sign contracts to use the site for purchasing. Therefore you will need to place salespeople in a variety of geographic locations. Investors need to know which locations you plan to start with, how you justify those choices, and what costs are associated with those choices.

3. *Internal computer systems.* In order for the company to run smoothly, a lot of thought and planning has to go into developing the internal systems to run the company. This ranges from selecting the hardware and software platforms to integrating them with field offices. The person in charge of this is typically the chief information officer and/or the director of information services. A plan that shows how the company will scale up and the cost for scaling up has to be thought out or the business can be crippled and disorganized.

4. *Finance.* Most venture capitalists are former commercial or investment bankers. They want to know what type of expense controls are in place so no one can embezzle their investment or spend money frivolously without receiving approval from more than one person in

management. Tracking income is just as important as tracking expenses. If you are developing a business exchange that brings buyers and sellers together and you are taking a piece of each transaction, a plan and controls need to be in place to track the deals that are consummated and how the exchange collects its revenue.

5. *Sales.* Many of the entrepreneurs I have worked with come from nonsales backgrounds and haven't given a lot of thought to how to create and implement a sales force. Even experienced entrepreneurs who have come from a brick-and-mortar company tend to underestimate the need for salespeople. They believe that an easy-to-use site, good customer service support, and spending heavily on marketing will be adequate. This section tells the investor what type of salespeople you plan to hire, when you plan to hire them, who will manage them, and what their goals and responsibilities will be.

6. *Marketing.* The business plan explains the marketing tactics you plan to use; the operating plan walks through how and when you plan to use what tactics. The order in which you plan to implement the various marketing tactics will impact your budget and the timing of potential sales. For example, if you start a business-to-consumer e-commerce company and you send out a direct mail piece announcing the launch of your site, then you can expect 10 to 15% of the recipients to visit your site, according to Bigfoot.com, one of the leading direct e-mail marketers. If you decide to give away a free T-shirt to the first 1,000 purchasers, that will trigger sales, which will affect the number of online sales/customer service support personnel you will need.

7. *Legal documents.* A lot of legal documents need to be developed for a variety of company interactions: employment, outsourced vendors, sales, advertising, vendor commissions, and assorted other contracts. The sample plan provided at the end of this chapter shows more than 10 legal documents that need to be developed. For example, a business-to-business website might have a contract with a media company to provide content and another contract with an order fulfillment house to ship product. You need to make a list of all the potential legal documents you need and hand them over to your attorney. For a company just starting out, you may be able to use Expert Software's Do-It-Yourself Lawyer *(www.expertsoftware.com)* to provide some

of the documents. Once this section is complete, you will end up going back to your business plan and increasing the cost for legal services.

8. *Vendor relationships.* Whether you are B2C (businesses that sell to consumers) or B2B, you need to have someone in charge of developing, maintaining, and policing vendor relationships. This section requires a description of the expertise, experience, and duties of the person responsible for vendor relationships, whom she reports to, and how those relationships will be implemented. For example, I am a partner in a venture that markets inventors. We had a salesperson to sell to inventors and corporations that would buy new products, but we didn't have anyone budgeted to develop a process and procedure to integrate and support inventors who were interested in participating in our site.

9. *Advisory board.* List types of expertise, types of experience, and desirable geographic locations you want in your advisory board members and how you plan to attract them. I didn't mention a board of directors, because if you are going for outside funding, the investors will have a major say in the composition of the board. For example, one of the ventures I am involved in is Createdolls.com. This site allows anyone to create a doll from scratch. Two of the advisory board members needed are a doll manufacturer and a girls' toys marketing expert.

10. *Retention.* It's one thing to do a great job in promoting and selling a product, but it is just as important to retain buyers and have them come back to buy more products. The cost of always finding new customers is high. You need to think about what steps you plan to take to retain customers. For example, if you are selling toys over the Internet, you might consider inviting 50 of your customers to your corporate headquarters or you might go to various cities to hold focus group meetings and ask customers what they like and don't like about your site. Once you have done that, post the results or e-mail them to all your customers to show them that you take customer input seriously.

Finally, the president of the company should be the person to write a draft of the operating plan because it provides him with a deeper understanding of the level of detail needed to run the business. Once the draft is complete, the leaders of each section of the operation should provide input into the plan before it goes to the investors.

Sample Plan

Here is a sample launch plan that an entrepreneur would provide to potential investors, board members, and her own staff. The plan should provide specifics, but should not get bogged down in minute detail. The following is a plan for a fictitious company called Worldfunding.com.

WEBSITE DEVELOPMENT

The chief operating officer, working with the chief information officer, will evaluate website developers to create the front of the website. The following spreadsheet describes the content that will be found on the website:

Section	Content and Technology	No. of Pgs.
Company		
Corporate History	Maximum five-paragraph description of company	1
Management	One-paragraph bios with link to e-mail	2
Contact Information	Map, addresses, directions, and telephone for regional offices	2
Security Information	Description of our security	1
Customer Service	Customer service policies and contact information	2
Funding		
Bank Application	Online application that feeds into an Oracle database that is sent to banks	5
Venture Capital Application	Online application that feeds into an Oracle database that is sent to VCs	5
Factoring Application	Online application that feeds into an Oracle database that is sent to factors	5
State Funding Application	Online application that feeds into an Oracle database that is sent to states	5

(continued)

Section	Content and Technology	No. of Pgs.
Business Exchange		
How to Sell a Business	Advice in HTML/Word written by experts	2
Online Valuation	Application for online business valuation	2
How to Structure a Deal	Advice in HTML/Word written by experts	2
Contract for Selling the Business	Application to sell business through Worldfunding	5
Worldfunding University		
Business Management	Online courses run through a partnership with online training company	5
Raising and Managing Capital	Online courses run through a partnership with online training company	5
Technology	Online courses run through a partnership with online training company	5
Business Support		
Accountants	Detailed RFP application link to database through *rfpMarket.com*	2
Attorneys	Detailed RFP application link to database through *rfpMarket.com*	2
Business Plans	Detailed RFP application link to database through *rfpMarket.com*	2
Human Resources	Detailed RFP application link to database through *rfpMarket.com*	2
Information Technology	Detailed RFP application link to database through *rfpMarket.com*	2
Marketing Plans	Detailed RFP application link to database through *rfpMarket.com*	2
Operations Plans	Detailed RFP application link to database through *rfpMarket.com*	2
Real Estate	Detailed RFP application link to database through *rfpMarket.com*	2
Sales Plans	Detailed RFP application link to database through *rfpMarket.com*	2
Website Development	Detailed RFP application link to database through *rfpMarket.com*	2

Section	Content and Technology	No. of Pgs.
Corporate Recruiting		
Finance	Detailed recruiting application linked to a recruiting partner	5
Management	Detailed recruiting application linked to a recruiting partner	5
Marketing	Detailed recruiting application linked to a recruiting partner	5
Human Resources	Detailed recruiting application linked to a recruiting partner	5
Information Technology	Detailed recruiting application linked to a recruiting partner	5
Sales	Detailed recruiting application linked to a recruiting partner	5
News		
Corporate Contract Awards	Paragraph description on who won various contracts	5
Financing Deals	Financing details reported in paragraph summaries stored on a database	5
Merger/Acquisition	Merger details reported in paragraph summaries stored on a database	5
Management Changes	Management changes within minority/Fortune 1000 stored on a database	5
Demographics	Links to Bureau of the Census for national and regional demographic information	5
Surveys	Internally generated surveys on various business topics stored on a database	5
Research Link	List of websites that make research easier	1
Bookstore		
Finance	Five books and one-paragraph summaries	1
Management	Five books and one-paragraph summaries	1
Marketing	Five books and one-paragraph summaries	1
Human Resources	Five books and one-paragraph summaries	1
Information Technology	Five books and one-paragraph summaries	1
Sales	Five books and one-paragraph summaries	1

CONTENT

Content will be subcontracted out to another media company. The company we are in conversations with to provide the content is run by a 10-year veteran of the *The Wall Street Journal.*

OFFICE ROLLOUT STRATEGY

We will initially rent office space in a shared office facility in Washington, D.C., and search for an appropriate corporate headquarters that will be physically close to potential influencers that will drive usage of the website. During the first year, we will engage real estate firms in each of the following targeted cities to look for suitable office space. (We will engage minority-owned firms to perform the search.) Here are the number of minority firms in those cities (according to a U.S. Bureau of the Census study) along with the months in which the sales offices will be rolled out:

Month	City	No. of Minority-Owned Firms
1	Washington–Baltimore	7,000
6	Atlanta	7,500
	Miami–Ft. Lauderdale	29,000
	New York	20,000
	Philadelphia–Wilmington	6,000
12	Boston	2,600
	Chicago	11,000
	Houston	7,000
	Los Angeles	40,000
24	Cleveland–Cincinnati	5,400
	Denver	4,100
	Minneapolis–St. Paul	1,300
	Kansas City–St. Louis	3,000
		143,900

INTERNAL COMPUTER SYSTEMS

We will hire a chief information officer (CIO) who has 10 years of internal systems development experience supporting more than 200 users in multiple locations. He or she will report to the chief operating officer. The responsibilities of the CIO will be as follows:

- Selecting hardware
- Selecting operating software
- Selecting telecommunications systems
- Selecting user software
- Assisting vice president of finance in selecting internal accounting software
- Selecting website hosting service

INTRANET DATABASES We will implement Oracle databases to track and store the following internal information:

- Government contacts
- Corporate contacts (telephone, e-mail, and address)
- Trade association contacts
- Other contacts
- Calendar of events
- Hiring
- Employment opportunities
- Health care applications
- Direct deposit applications
- Vacation applications
- Illness notifications
- Requisition applications

WEBSITE DATABASES We will implement Oracle databases to track and store the following:

- Bank financing applications
- Business brokerage buyer and seller applications
- Corporate contract award news
- Educational offerings
- Employment recruiting applications
- Factoring applications
- Mergers and acquisitions news
- Worldfunding corporate contact information by office
- Venture financing applications
- Venture financing news
- State financing applications
- State financing news

FINANCE

We will hire a vice president of finance who has a minimum of 15 years of accounting and finance experience. He or she will report to the chief operating officer. This person will be responsible for the following:

- Setting up lines of credit
- Setting up payroll
- Setting up internal expense controls
- Setting up controls to track revenue
- Working with each department to set up budgets
- Interacting with accounting firms
- Interacting with shareholders
- Overseeing human resources

SALES

Initially, sales will be overseen by the chairman/CEO. Within six months of development of the site, we will have identified and hired a vice president of sales. The vice president of sales will have a minimum of 15 years of sales experience and have managed a national sales force. He or she will report to the chairman/CEO.

Business Development

We will hire four business development directors in the first year. Those directors will start out in Washington, D.C. They should have the following characteristics:

- Minimum four-year college degree
- Minimum four years of sales experience
- Preferred background working with a trade association
- Be well organized
- Be good networkers
- Be ambitious
- Have great communication skills

DUTIES   Their duties will include the following:

- Develop alliances with local chambers of commerce, trade associations, banks, and accounting and law firms.
- Co-sponsor seminars with alliance partners on financing and growing a business.
- Promote various corporate offerings.

SALES TRAINING PROCESS   Each business development director will be put through a two-day training program. The curriculum will include the following:

- Mission and goals of Worldfunding
- Review of corporate operating procedures
- Review of key contacts in their market

- Procedure for setting up regional partnerships for seminars
- Review of how the website works and practice using the site
- Training on how to teach someone to use Worldfunding
- Procedure for how to handle unhappy users of the website
- Review of director's goals with vice president of sales

DEVELOPING SALES OPPORTUNITIES

The following will be done to initiate sales opportunities:

- Marketing department will create appropriate letters for each minority marketplace. They will be signed by the business development director of each minority market.
- Business development directors will network at regional chambers of commerce, trade associations, and business events.
- Business development directors will develop relationships with targeted influencers to generate leads.

MARKETING

During the period our website is being developed, we will begin to populate our database with the following types of contacts: primary users and influencers.

PRIMARY USERS   This group will have the following titles:

- Owners
- Chairman
- CEO
- Chief operating officer
- Chief financial officer
- Vice president of finance

INFLUENCERS   This group is made up of the following:

- Accountants
- Attorneys
- Bank branch managers and loan officers
- Chamber of commerce program managers
- Trade association program managers
- Chamber of commerce president
- Trade association president
- Congressional represenatives
- Senators
- Governors
- Mayors of targeted cities
- Directors of commerce for targeted cities
- Directors of commerce for states
- Venture capitalists
- Executive directors of private investor groups
- Media (business writers, television and radio commentators)

Our marketing strategy will be implemented in six phases. Our marketing mission in our first year is to develop brand awareness in four major markets and test the marketing tactics that provide the best results.

Phase 1: We will hire a public relations firm with strong minority media contacts and hold a press conference in New York to announce the launch of Worldfunding. This launch will occur once our website is operational and has been tested. Our public relations firm will set up a series of interviews with the media and speeches with targeted user groups.

Phase 2: We will advertise our site initially in the Washington–Baltimore market through local newspapers, through direct mail pieces, and through a series of seminars on how to raise capital and buy and sell businesses.

Phase 3: Once all the bugs are worked out of our system, we will launch in three major cities and benchmark the results against our business plan.

Phase 4: At the end of the first year, we will implement a mass traditional mailing and opt-in e-mail that feature pictures, descriptions, and links to our website.

Phase 5: During the fourth quarter of our first year, we will begin to send a weekly e-mail about deals that were consummated, changes in management, and additions to the website.

Phase 6: We will partner with a national media company to develop a national magazine and radio and television shows focused on financing and selling minority-related businesses.

LEGAL CONTRACTS

We will use an outside law firm in conjunction with an industry expert to develop online applications for the following areas:

- *Site-related contracts:*
  - Bank financing
  - Business brokerage
  - Employment recruiting
  - Factoring
  - Venture financing
  - State financing
  - Sponsorship
  - Advertising
  - Trade shows
- *Worldfunding internal contracts:*
  - Advisory board stock grant agreements
  - Employment contracts
  - Shareholder agreements

Vendor Relationships

We will hire an individual who has 10 to 15 years of Community Reinvestment Act commercial banking experience to be our vice president of bank relationships. This individual will be responsible for the following:

- Developing criteria for our expectations from banks that want to receive leads from Worldfunding.

- Developing a list of banks that fit our criteria.

- Developing a staff of former Community Reinvestment Act commercial bank officers to develop banking relationships.

- Introducing our marketing staff to partner with bank marketing staffs to develop joint seminars.

- Developing and overseeing an advisory board of banks to allow them input into Worldfunding operations.

Advisory Boards

We will form regional advisory boards for each minority group. One member from each of those groups will serve on a national advisory board. The regional advisory boards, which will be composed of no more than 10 individuals, will meet quarterly. The national advisory board will meet annually. Advisory board members must have been in business for a minimum of five years. Their duties will be as follows:

- To provide input to Worldfunding on how our services could be improved.

- To promote our service to regional businesses.

- To participate in regional seminars on financing, business growth strategies, and buying and selling of businesses.

- To review the performance of regional directors.

Retention

There are two areas regarding retention we have to be concerned with. The first is retaining customers and the second is retaining employees.

CUSTOMER RETENTION   To ensure that users find enough value in the service to come back and recommend it to others, we will execute the following:

- We will hire an outside consultant after the site is in operation to interview 25 users who have applied for loans, tried to sell their businesses, or tried to find a consultant.

- The COO will conduct focus groups of 10 to 20 business executives in each city to understand how we can improve our service.

- A complaints e-mail box will be set up and the COO's assistant will compile a list of complaints to be reviewed by management and responded to by the COO.

- At the six-month and one-year anniversaries of the company, an outside consulting firm will conduct interviews with 100 users over a 30-day period to obtain insights into whether service is meeting their needs and how we can improve it.

- Management will ask each regional board and the national advisory board to grade the company's performance.

EMPLOYEE RETENTION   Our plan to attract and retain the best employees is the following:

- Provide stock options to all employees whether they are full- or part-time, based on a percentage of salary. We want part-time employees to be as focused and work as hard as full-time employees.

- Provide full health care benefits for individuals and their families.

- Provide off-site training.

- Provide two weeks of paid vacation. People who are with the company for a minimum of five years will receive an additional two days of vacation for every year up to a total of 25 days. We believe that our employees will be working more than 50-hour weeks, so we want to reward them.

- Provide a day off for their birthdays.

• Provide $100 per year to each employee for business book and magazine purchases.

CHAPTER SUMMARY

Count on investors, private and institutional, to ask for an operating plan. Make sure your operating plan covers the following parts of your business:

• Website development
• Sales
• Marketing
• Retention
• Vendor relationships
• Legal documents
• Internal computer systems
• Advisory board
• Office rollout
• Finance

Have your accountant, lawyer, and potential or current employees scrutinize it. Ask them to e-mail you questions about areas that they think remain to be covered as well as areas that are covered with an approach that is unclear or wrong.

4

How to Write a
Marketing and Sales Plan

The first document a venture capitalist needs to review is the company's business plan. Once the venture capitalists decide they like the business model, then they ask for an operating plan so they can understand how the company intends to roll out its business. The third document they ask for is a marketing and sales plan so they can get a deeper understanding of how the company plans to build buyer awareness, attract customers, and close sales.

To explain the difference between marketing and sales, let me offer an analogy. If you can, picture World War II's D-Day invasion with the battleships firing their cannon and the aircraft carriers sending their planes into battle. The battleships and aircraft are the marketing department. They are letting friends (customers) and foes (competition) know what they offer and how they offer it. In this battle example, the battleships and aircraft are announcing that the American, British, and Canadian forces have arrived and their products are superior weapons and tougher fighting men.

The ground troops storming the beach are like the sales forces deployed after the battleships and airplanes have promoted their arrival. The troops' mission, like a sales group's mission, is to close the sale and capture the territory.

The marketing and sales plan provides in-depth details of how to execute the ideas mentioned in the business and operating plan. The marketing and sales plan should be put together by whoever is heading marketing and sales. Most companies have one person handling both functions. It has been my experience that most presidents of companies don't understand the difference between marketing and sales so they hire someone with experience at building sales organizations and very little understanding of marketing. The company, if it can afford it, would be best served for the long term by hiring a vice president of sales and a vice president of marketing and having them collaborate on a marketing and sales plan.

ELEMENTS OF A MARKETING AND SALES PLAN

A marketing and sales plan typically includes the following sections:

- *Executive summary.* The executive summary doesn't have to give a section-by-section overview, but it should describe what the reader will find in the plan.

- *Mission statement.* The mission statement tells the reader what the marketing and sales departments are going to try to accomplish.

- *Competitive advantage.* The only way you can convince customers to choose your website over another is to explain why you are better. You need to articulate your competitive advantages. Competitive advantages could be anything from exclusive partnerships to the ease of use of the site itself.

- *Objectives.* The objectives section should list definitive goals such as, but not limited to, the number of new customers, the number of publications the company plans to get coverage in, and the amount of sales it expects to generate, both long and short term.

- *Target market.* Everyone in the organization and the investors need to know who the targeted users of the website are. A record retailer may be targeting girls ages 10 through 15 to buy specific girl singers. An online employment site may be targeting human resource directors and information technology managers of Fortune 1000 companies or presidents and recruiters of small IT companies. The point is that marketing needs to know whom the company is selling to in order to pick the appropriate marketing vehicles to build site awareness. The sales team needs to know who the targeted buyer is to determine the level of experience that the salespeople they are hiring will need.

- *Marketing strategies.* Step by step, describe how the company will use postcards, traditional mail, e-mail, newsletters, print advertising, banner advertising, sponsorships, and trade shows to build name recognition among potential users of the site.

- *Sales strategies.* This section provides details on the steps the sales team will use to bring in customers. In the B2C space it will range from signing online and offline strategic partners to developing affiliate programs. B2B companies use the same strategies as B2C ones, but they also have to deploy salespeople to visit corporate clients and demonstrate how their sites work and sign clients to contracts to use their sites.

- *Retention program.* The operating plan described the steps that would be taken to retain customers. The marketing and sales plan describes the roles marketing and sales will play in retention. For example, the company will hire an outside firm to conduct focus groups with customers to hear what customers think about the way the company is marketing itself, and what sales tactics work and do not work.

- *Personnel.* The marketing and sales departments need to describe the type and number of professionals they will need in order to execute their parts of the plan. For example, the marketing department may have thought that one person could cover three cities, but if they then realize that the amount of activity each city requires to generate sales warrants having one marketing director per city, that will affect the marketing department's budget and the company's rollout strategy.

- *Competition.* Marketing and sales need to be aware of what the competition is doing and have a plan for how they will cancel out or neutralize the competition's marketing and sales initiatives. For example, one of my clients found out that its primary competitor was signing a deal with one of the Big Three broadcasting companies. My client went to the broadcasting company and offered a better deal than the competition. This was such a great blow to the competition that the competitor offered to merge with my client.

• *Launch plan.* The business plan gave an overview of what each department's role in the launch of the website would be, but the marketing and sales plan goes into greater detail on who will do what and when. Writing this part of the plan is a great exercise because it allows the marketing and sales leadership to manage their budgets better, get a handle on what their future needs will be, and provide ideas for improving what each department plans to do.

• *Financials.* Each group has to map out how it plans to spend its portion of whatever money the company raises and the return on that investment that each group feels is realistic. Seeing numbers on paper and matching them with what each group plans to do provides a reality check on what the company can accomplish with the dollars it plans to raise.

Similar to the other plans you have written for your investors, the marketing and sales plan has a life expectancy of a year at the most, possibly less than six months. Experienced investors realize that markets and business are in a constant state of change and revision, so making changes along the way is to be expected. Investors would be surprised and concerned if adjustments weren't made to roll with changes in the market. The following sample marketing and sales plan illustrates these concepts.

MARKETING AND SALES PLAN FOR
PENNSYLVANIA FUNDING
PHILADELPHIA METRO

EXECUTIVE SUMMARY

This marketing and sales plan focuses on how we plan to build our brand and implement our sales force in Pennsylvania. If we are successful in Pennsylvania, we will roll out our concept to other states.

Pennsylvania Funding's Current Customer Base

Pennsylvania Funding's customers typically have incomes of $500,000 to $2 million, and according to the U.S. Bureau of the Census, the size of our target market is 29,000 companies that have full-time employees.

Pennsylvania Funding's strengths and achievements include:

- First website to provide access to multiple financial institutions to find debt lending and equity financing.
- Seventy-five years of loan and equity experience.
- Exclusive agreements with state, county, and city websites to provide links from their websites to ours to promote funding opportunities.

Present

Currently, we are developing the first phase of the website and expect to launch the site for trial use within 60 days.

Goals

Short Term: Pennsylvania Funding/Philadelphia Metro's goal is to bring in $1 million worth of new business in 2000.

Long Term: Pennsylvania Funding/Philadelphia Metro's goal is to bring in $50 million in revenue by 2005.

MISSION STATEMENT

This section allows us to state what we believe our mission is.

The mission of Pennsylvania Funding is to provide the largest number of online funding sources to small and medium-sized businesses in the state of Pennsylvania.

COMPETITIVE ADVANTAGE

- First to market.
- Largest database of funding sources.
- Exclusive agreements with state, county, and local governments to promote the site.
- Exclusive agreements with state and regional chambers of commerce and other business associations to promote the site.

OBJECTIVES

Short Term: 1998–2000

Financial:

- Develop $1 million worth of new business in 2001.
- Develop $10 million worth of new business and develop $10 million from existing customers in 2002.
- Develop $20 million worth of new business and develop $40 million from existing customers in 2003.

Visibility:

- Run six seminars that attract 180 new prospects.
- Appear six times in regional newspapers.
- Write a monthly column for one to two regional publications.

Personnel:

- Hire two business development people.
- Hire full-time marketing directors to focus on specific geographic segments and marketing manager to oversee implementation and support directors.

Long Term: 2001–2003

Financial:

- Develop $30 million worth of new business and develop $60 million from existing customers in 2004.

- Develop $60 million worth of new business and develop $90 million from existing customers in 2006.

- Develop $90 million worth of new business and develop $120 million from existing customers in 2008.

Visibility:

- Run 10 seminars per year that attract 300 new prospects.

- Appear 26 times in regional newspapers.

- Write a monthly column for four to five regional newspapers.

TARGET MARKET(S)

This section provides a profile of our target industries and the names of specific companies in each industry.

Overall Profile

- Revenues of $1 million or more

- Fewer than 100 employees

MARKETING STRATEGIES

This section provides information on how we will market the company to prospects and current customers.

Marketing Package

- Brochure on services

- List of companies that have received funding

- White paper on growing and financing a company
- Client endorsement letters

Presentation Materials (PowerPoint Presentation)

Replicate selected collateral material in PowerPoint (laptop) and on foils. Include info specific to the prospect.

Joint Venture/Lead Partners

- Arthur Andersen
- Asher & Company
- BDO Seidman

Sponsorships/Memberships

- Chemical Manufacturers Association
- Chester County Chamber of Commerce
- Delaware Valley Manufacturers' Resource Center

Mass Mailing to Target Audiences

- Postcards including website
- Letters to prospects that include only a white paper

Trade Shows

- Chamber of Commerce
- Small Business Administration

Events to Be Attended (by Top Executives)

- Bauer Awards at Franklin Institute
- Borrower's Ball (Philadelphia Free Library)
- Enterprise Awards (Eastern Technology Council)

Initial Sample Letter

Dear Mr. Smith:

I recently joined Pennsylvania Funding as a partner in the Philadelphia office. Part of my responsibilities is to facilitate the flow of information on using the Internet. We would like to invite you to participate in a panel discussion on how you use the Internet for raising capital. The attendees will be high-level executives who oversee their companies' Internet strategies and deployments.

By way of background on Pennsylvania Funding, we are a startup company whose management is made up of former bank loan officers and venture capitalists. We have been involved with over $2 billion in financings over the past 10 years.

Please visit our website at *www.pennsylvaniafunding.com*. I will call your office within the next week to discuss your participation in our seminar series.

Sincerely,

Marc Kramer
Partner

Success Seminar Series

This was touched on already, but developing a quality seminar series will raise our visibility and put us in a position to attract and retain business.

Newsletter

We need to develop a bimonthly or monthly newsletter that is both electronic and in paper form. The newsletter, which would augment the white papers, would include the following:

- Tips on how to write a business plan, operating plan, and marketing plan
- Tips on how to present the company to investors
- Tips on how to recruit quality employees
- Interviews with business leaders

SALES STRATEGIES

This section describes how we plan to sell our services and product.

The steps we will take to attract new customers are as follows:

1. **Identify prospects.** Prospects in this plan are classified by the verticals in which they participate and are listed by name.

2. **Send letters to prospects.** We will send a one-page letter to each prospective company along with our information packet.

3. **Follow up with a telephone call.** Each person who receives a letter from us will be contacted within 10 days of his or her package being mailed. The person following up will say the following:

   Good morning, I am Marc Kramer, a partner in the Philadelphia office of Pennsylvania Funding. I sent you a package last week and I wanted to make sure you received it. I would like to invite you to lunch to discuss your participation in our Internet seminar series. What day and time would work for you?

4. **Arrange visit(s).** When we visit target companies, we will be dressed in conservative suits and white shirts and blouses. We want to come off as friendly and professional. We will bring a laptop that has a PowerPoint presentation and a link to our website to demonstrate how our Pennsylvania Funding works.

5. **Develop a seminar series.** We will develop a six-part seminar series with banks, accounting firms, and chambers of commerce for each minority group. We will put together an advisory board that will select the topics to be discussed. As an example, financial institutions could use the following topics:

   - Future of online banking
   - Finding quality technology people
   - Differentiating your website from the competition
   - Smart cards and the Internet

6. **Close sales.** To close sales we will do the following:

   - Research the company and industry we are going after.
   - Ask good questions and do a lot of listening.

- Encourage customers to visit our website and to speak with other businesspeople who have used the site.
- Make sure we follow up to find out if their experience with our site was a good one.

RETENTION PROGRAM

Pennsylvania Funding will have a formalized retention program.

- Contact our clients once a month to find out if they are happy with our service.
- Provide articles related to business.
- Invite new clients to meet with the Pennsylvania Funding advisory board once a year.
- Host a yearly event as a way to thank clients.
- Buy four season tickets to the Walnut Street Theatre to network with big clients in order to develop long-term relationships.
- Have Pennsylvania Funding's website feature links to sites that have information related to the interactive industry.
- Once a year have a formal review by each client. Half the clients will be interviewed in July and the other half in August. Each partner will interview the other partner's clients in order to get an impartial evaluation.

Personnel

Sales/consultants: We need to hire two people who have the following experience, traits, and skills:

- Three to five years of banking and/or venture capital experience
- Minimum of a college degree, but preferably an MBA
- Use of the Internet
- Good writing and verbal communication skills
- Personable
- Team player

Note: We want someone who can talk about the company intelligently if no one else is available.

COMPETITION

This section focuses on the strengths and weaknesses of Pennsylvania Funding's primary competitors. This helps Pennsylvania Funding position itself with prospects and helps employees focus on what makes Pennsylvania Funding unique.

Competitor	Strengths	Weaknesses
USFunding.com	International Cash rich Stock rich Good reputation Great client list	Expensive

LAUNCH PLAN

This section describes how we plan to launch our marketing and sales program. The launch program is broken down by month and action items.

Month	Action Items
January	Approve sales/marketing plan. Run advertisement for two full-time sales consultants. Run advertisement for one secretary/office manager. Line up joint venture partners for seminars. Send letters and packets to five companies on target list per week. Visit two target companies.
February	Hire two full-time sales consultants. Hire one secretary/office manager. Select and approve topics for seminars. Send letters and packets to five companies on target list per week. Visit four target companies. Develop a bimonthly newsletter.

Month	Action Items
March	Run first event. Send letters and packets to five companies on target list per week. Visit eight target companies. Put together bimonthly newsletter.
April	Run second event. Send letters and packets to five companies on target list per week. Visit eight target companies. Mail newsletter.
May	Run third event. Send letters and packets to five companies on target list per week. Visit eight target companies. Work on second edition of newsletter.
June	Run fourth event. Send letters and packets to five companies on target list per week. Visit eight target companies. Complete second edition of newsletter.
July	Run fifth event. Send letters and packets to five companies on target list per week. Visit eight target companies. Mail second edition of newsletter.
August	Send letters and packets to five companies on target list per week. Visit eight target companies. Begin planning for 2002. Begin third newsletter.
September	Run sixth event. Send letters and packets to five companies on target list per week. Visit eight target companies. Edit third newsletter.
October	Run seventh event. Send letters and packets to five companies on target list per week. Visit eight target companies. Mail third newsletter.

Month	Action Items
November	Run eighth event.
	Send letters and packets to five companies on target list per week.
	Visit eight target companies.
	Begin fourth newsletter.
December	Run ninth event.
	Send letters and packets to five companies on target list per week.
	Visit eight target companies.
	Edit fourth newsletter (to be mailed in January).

FINANCIALS

Years	Yr 1	Yr 2	Yr 3	Yr 4	Yr5
Revenue	$1,000,000	$3,000,000	$6,000,000	$9,000,000	$13,500,000
Expense					
Partner	$90,000	$94,500	$99,225	$104,186	$109,396
Senior Consultants	$100,000	$105,000	$110,250	$115,763	$121,551
Support Staff	$25,000	$26,250	$27,563	$28,941	$30,388
Tax and Benefits	$53,750	$56,438	$59,259	$62,222	$65,333
Packet Mailing	$1,500	$1,625	$1,750	$1,875	$2,000
Seminar Mailing	$640	$1,536	$1,536	$1,536	$1,536
Seminar Cost	$3,000	$3,000	$3,000	$3,000	$3,000
CD-ROM Development Cost	$25,000	0	0	0	0
Travel	$18,000	$21,600	$42,000	$48,000	$75,600
Telephone	$3,600	$4,500	$9,000	$10,500	$16,800
Memberships	$5,000	$5,000	$5,000	$5,000	$5,000
Total	$325,490	$319,449	$358,583	$381,023	$430,603
Profit (Loss)	$674,510	$2,680,551	$5,641,417	$8,618,977	$13,069,347
Notes					
Partner	$90,000	$94,500	$99,225	$104,186	$109,396
Pay Raise (%)	1	1.05	1.05	1.05	1.05

Years	Yr 1	Yr 2	Yr 3	Yr 4	Yr5
Senior Consultants	$100,000	$105,000	$110,250	$115,763	$121,551
Pay Raise (%)	1	1.05	1.05	1.05	1.05
No. of Consultants	2	2	4	4	6
Support Staff	$25,000	$26,250	$27,563	$28,941	$30,388
Pay Raise (%)	1	1.05	1.05	1.05	1.05
No. of Staff	1	2	2	3	4
Tax and Benefits (%)	0.25	0.25	0.25	0.25	0.25
Packet Mailing	500	500	500	500	500
Postage	$3	$3.25	$3.5	$3.75	$4
Seminar Mailing	200	400	400	400	400
No. of Seminars	10	12	12	12	12
Postage/Fax	$0.32	$0.32	$0.32	$0.32	$0.32
Seminar Cost	$300	$300	$300	$300	$300
No. of Seminars	10	10	10	10	10
CD-ROM Development Cost	$25,000	$0	$0	$0	$0
Travel	$500	$600	$700	$800	$900
No. of People	3	3	5	5	7
No. of Months	12	12	12	12	12
Telephone	$100	$125	$150	$175	$200
No. of People	3	3	5	5	7
No. of Months	12	12	12	12	12
Memberships	$5,000	$5,000	$5,000	$5,000	$5,000

CHAPTER SUMMARY

The employees and the investors both need to see a written plan on how the company intends to bring in revenue through the use of marketing and sales strategy and the execution. It is important to focus on the following when articulating your marketing and sales plan.

- Target market—the industries that would be most receptive to what you offer.

- Individual professionals—the titles of the individuals in the targeted companies.

- Marketing tools—deciding whether you are going to use direct mail, opt-in e-mail, radio, television, banner advertising, online and offline newsletters, seminars, and trade shows.

- Strategic partnerships—interviewing and evaluating potential partners that can bring in sales or pass on sales leads.

- Budget—the amount of money everyone has to work with to execute the marketing and sales plan.

Everyone has to understand and buy into the marketing and sales plan for it to be effective.

5

HIRING A BLUE CHIP
MANAGEMENT TEAM

When an investor first looks at a business plan, he focuses on three sections of the plan: the concept, the revenue projections, and what most venture capitalists say is the most important part of the plan, the team responsible for building and managing the company.

Building a management team is like building a championship team in sports. You need to find individuals who are talented, willing to work 12 hours a day, and able to check their egos at the door for the greater good of the organization.

AFFORDING THE BEST

Whether you are recruiting employees yourself or using an executive recruiter, go after the best people. Don't worry about how much money they make. A client of mine was asked by a venture capitalist who he thought were the two or three most well-connected people who could make his venture a success. My client named one individual who was making $5 million a year. The venture capitalist told my client to call the superstar and ask if he would be willing to have dinner and hear about my client's venture.

The superstar agreed to meet and hear about my client's venture. The client and the venture capitalist told the superstar over dinner what their plans were and what type of employees were needed to make the venture a success. At the end of the evening, the superstar said he would be interested because he had never been involved in a startup. My client said he could offer him only a small salary, but would give him 5% of the company phased in over two years if he joined. The superstar joined.

Signing a superstar in business is like signing a superstar in sports. When Shaquille O'Neal, the Los Angeles Lakers' all-star center, joined the team, other star players and coaches wanted to join. The superstar my client signed helped to attract other industry stars, and to date the company has raised $70 million. Without the superstar, the business wouldn't have had the credibility it needed to attract investors.

Before you begin hiring anyone, develop a profile of the type of person you want to work with. Over the years, I used the following checklist to develop my team:

1. *Entrepreneurial.* Anyone who requires a lot of structure and support staff is not going to survive in an entrepreneurial company because he or she would have a hard time adjusting to the lack of resources inherent in any startup. I try to recruit people who have been involved in other startups or have started something internally at a large corporation.

2. *Self-motivated.* Many startups fail because the people hired were used to being micromanaged in big organizations and couldn't adjust to making decisions on their own. Managers in a startup need to coordinate and communicate with other managers in the organization, but they need to run their group as if it were their own company. They also have to be willing to put in long hours. Startups are not involved in marathons; they are in sprints. Everyone you recruit had better be working on high octane or you will either get run over by the competition or run out of money before you reach the finish line.

3. *Avoid arrogance.* Many very bright people believe their understanding, knowledge, and opinion are infallible. This type of person can be a cancer to the organization because he wil underestimate the competition and stifle the growth of everyone around him. Other smart people won't want to work for him and only weak people will stay.

4. *Loyalty.* You have to know that the people you hire will not run when the going gets rough and that they won't put their needs above the organization's. Make sure you do a thorough background check on everyone you hire and find out if they are loyal to their employers or just loyal to whoever pays them the most. I once had an employee who was being courted by a competitor. This person had intimate knowledge of our sales and marketing strategies. One day, after everyone had left for the evening, a fax came addressed to the employee from the competitor offering this employee a position. Unfortunately for the employee, someone picked up the fax and forwarded it to me. I asked the employee if she was happy and if there were any problems. The employee told me she was very happy. Finally, I told the employee I knew she was talking to a competitor, and the employee left my office, grabbed her stuff, and exited.

5. *Honesty and integrity.* I once interviewed a prospective employee who had started and failed in business. It didn't bother me that he failed, because everyone who is successful has failed at some point. What bothered me was that he laughed when describing how he got his landlord to accept his signature on a lease instead of insisting that his wife co-sign. If his wife had co-signed, then they would have been personally liable, thereby removing any opportunity the landlord had of collecting the rent owed to him if he sued. I am a firm believer that your word is your bond and you do not try to take advantage of other people. The landlord trusted him. I decided not to hire him because I thought he lacked honesty and integrity.

6. *Thrives on pressure.* The words *pressure* and *startup* go together like peanut butter and jelly. Every day you are battling competition for a piece of someone's budget, you are trying to prove your site is better than the competition's, you never have enough money or resources to do what you want. Some people thrive on it and others crumble.

7. *Smarter than I am.* I have worked with entrepreneurs whose insecurity about themselves led them to hire inferior talent. When investors met the team, it was obvious that the entrepreneur felt it was more important to be the star and the one everyone comes to for direction than it was to have a team of people who could run on their own. I tell everyone I hire

that if someone doesn't try to recruit them away from me within three years, then I have made a poor choice.

8. *Experience.* Many entrepreneurs try to get people right out of college who will work long hours. The problem with that thinking is that the learning curve is long and it will cost you a lot of money to train them. Startup companies can't afford to hire inexperienced people in critical positions such as sales, marketing, or finance. But you can hire people right out of college for positions in information systems because their programming skills may be just as good, if not better, than someone who has been out of school.

9. *Respects money.* Money is the most precious asset in a startup and the hardest to come by. At any company I am involved in, I always tell the president and his staff that the money just raised may be the last dollar they make until they show revenue and possibly profits. Spend every dollar judiciously. Employees who are overly worried about the look of the company's office space and spend money lavishly on clients at expensive restaurants will eventually put you out of business and then they will move on to the next sucker.

10. *Good recruiter.* Hire quality employees who have friends in other organizations that they can recruit. An employee who is a good recruiter can save the company a fortune in executive recruiting fees and will make sure that the person recruited will have an easy transition.

HOW TO FIND THE BEST

Finding star players can take a lot of time if you don't have a big network. There are several ways to find top management talent.

- *Past associates.* If you have worked in a large company, you may have reported to or worked with someone you feel is a good fit. Don't hesitate to speak with that person about your concept and see if she is interested or has someone else to recommend.

- *Outplacement firms.* Few entrepreneurs, unless they have worked with large companies and were downsized, know about outplacement firms. Outplacement firms are used by companies who are letting go of managers because of financial circumstances or because the executive didn't fit into their culture. These firms provide space and career counseling for their clients. When professionals are put in outplacement, the first thing they are required to do is develop a resume. Anyone who is interested in meeting outplaced professionals can either contact an outplacement firm or go to its website. The biggest outplacement firms internationally are Right Management Consultants *(www.right.com)*, Lee Hecht Harrison *(www.leehecht.com)*, Manchester Associates *(www.manchesterusa.com)*, and Drake Beam & Morrison *(www.dbm.com)*.

- *Media.* This may surprise you, but I contact reporters at publications that cover e-commerce such as *B2B (www.netb2b.com)*, *The Industry Standard (www.thestandard.com)*, and *Interactive Week (www.interactiveweek.com)* to ask which executives impress them the most. Reporters are very insightful and they see who thinks well on their feet.

- *Executive search firms.* There are times when your network of contacts isn't enough and you need professional assistance. A good executive recruiter can help you attract capital by recruiting the best people. Look for executive recruiters who have national, not just regional, contacts. Three internationally respected recruiting firms that every venture capitalist knows are Heidrick & Struggles *(www.h-s.com)*, Spencer Stuart *(www.spencerstuart.com)*, and Korn/Ferry International *(www.kornferry.com)*.

USING AN EXECUTIVE RECRUITER

A great executive recruiter doesn't have to be with a large international firm. The advantage of hiring a name-brand executive recruiting firm is that it is easier to attract top-tier candidates, and it makes a statement to investors about your focus on attracting the best people. To get insights into the business of executive recruiting, I interviewed Ken Kring, a current partner at Heidrick & Struggles and a former partner at Spencer Stuart.

Ken Kring is the managing partner of the Philadelphia office of Heidrick & Struggles. Since 1985, he has successfully recruited more than 200 senior-level executives and board directors for leading corporations as well as for emerging and privately held companies in various industry sectors. A particular focus of his practice is serving clients during pre- and post-IPO organizations. A graduate of Stanford University with a B.A. in psychology, Ken holds a master's degree in public and private management from the Yale School of Management.

How should an entrepreneur evaluate executive recruiters before hiring one?

Executive recruiters should be only one of a menu of services for talent. The entrepreneur should use an executive recruiter as a court of last resort. He should use an executive recruiter after he has exhausted his network. When selecting a search firm in this market you need to shop for a recruiter who has relevant experience in specific requirements of the industry and function you are attempting to recruit for. You want someone who doesn't just appeal to you, but can get the job done, someone with relevant experience and strong industry contacts.

What is the process a recruiter goes through when evaluating prospective candidates?

Most firms are using some sort of competency assessment model. Maybe there are four to eight key characteristics that the client and recruiter agree on. They are specific behavioral and experiential achievements that can be measured and qualified in an interview and corroborated through references. The interview will take anywhere from one hour to three hours. As soon as it is practical, the recruiter will contact the candidate's references and speak to people who can comment on the candidate's experience and capabilities compared to the competencies required in the job.

How much time do you spend getting to know the CEO and the company's culture before beginning your assignment?

It is a continuity of events. It may begin with a relationship that predates the specific engagement. Many times our clients are people we have worked for before. On an individual engagement we will spend a couple of hours initially to get comfortable with each other and then will spend another couple of hours with his/her top-level staff. We will also pull down public domain information about the company. Like in teaching, there is twice as much preparation as time in the classroom.

How important is it that recruiters understand the industry they are recruiting for?

I think it is most important in order to get a fast start. It probably saves a search two weeks to a month. I can start in an industry I know nothing about and figure out the outstanding candidates and what their hot buttons are without knowing the business. However, most clients can't afford to wait for the recruiter to get oriented and, therefore, knowing the industry becomes important.

What are the traits of a great recruiter?

Judgment, initiative, energy, persistence, interpersonal skills, business savvy, intellectual curiosity, intelligence, and ultimately, closing skills. Great recruiters are very task oriented. Finding and closing on a superb candidate is a very purposeful event.

What is the typical fee entrepreneurs can expect to pay?

One-third of the first year's cash compensation of the candidate. For pre-IPO companies it is now more often one-third of "the deal"—one-third of the cash compensation and one-third of the vested stock options.

Do you take any part of your compensation in stock or options?

In most cases we do. So let's say a candidate receives 100,000 options, of which one-quarter, or 25,000, will vest in the first year. We receive a third of that number in warrants and we sell those warrants when there is a capital event.

What guarantee do recruiters typically give in the event the new hire isn't a fit or decides to leave within the first year?

We give a warranty that the search is redone at no additional fee except for expenses. This typically isn't in a contract, but the entrepreneur should ask for it.

What types of personalities and skills do you usually look for in prospective candidates who fit best with entrepreneurial companies?

Many of our candidates now come from traditional brick-and-mortar companies. The most important transitional quality is that they can try to survive in a fast-moving company. We look for relevant achievement, flexibility, ego control, basic intelligence, and the ability to understand and the willingness to adapt to what they are getting into. We look for relevant accomplishments.

How important is it to have gone to an elite school to be on the radar screen of a recruiter?

At entry level, going to a prestige school is very important. For experienced people, it is irrelevant.

What types of entrepreneurs have you met that you turned down as clients?

Entrepreneurs who are unwilling or unable to forge a value-added partnership. They think we are a vendor and think we will do as they tell us to do. They will get into a discourse with us that underappreciates our experience and resources. We would not work with people who we think are too arrogant, too dumb, too busy, or too distracted for us to partner with effectively.

What typical salary and stock compensation does a CEO *receive?*

Once the money comes in, to get a good CEO, you can expect to pay cash of $200,000 to $300,000 and 5 to 10% of the company depending on where they are in terms of dilution. There is another 5 to 10% set aside for the rest of the team.

What are the typical salary and stock compensation for the other top managers (VP of sales, marketing, HR, *and finance)?*

They typically would receive $150,000 to $250,000 after significant rounds of financing and also receive 1% or so of the company.

How long does it usually take to find quality people?

The difficult part isn't finding, it is securing. Searches take between four and six months. They can be done more quickly if the client and recruiter know whom they want. If it takes more than six months, it usually is because of a turndown or the company wants to wait for a particular candidate. It usually takes a little over a month to survey and make a list of possible candidates, two months for all the interviews to take place, and another month for the courtship and to get the person on board.

Do you ever recruit someone who is unemployed?

Yes, all the time. There is no longer a stigma about being out of work. People are unemployed for a variety of reasons that may or may not have anything to do with their skill and usually have to do with external events beyond their control.

Before you hire any employees you should work with an attorney who specializes in employee contracts. This is extremely important for Internet-related companies, because the value of the business is the employees. If a competitor is able to recruit the head of sales of another company, this could cripple the targeted employer's former company. Here is an interview with a leading labor attorney who has worked with such companies as I-Village.

EMPLOYMENT AGREEMENTS

Jeffrey I. Pasek is chair of the Labor and Employment Law Department for Cozen and O'Connor, a national law firm based in Philadelphia. Before coming to the firm, he was a member of the firm Cohen, Shapiro, Polisher, Shiekman and Cohen, where he practiced since 1976 and served as chair of its Labor and Employment Law Department and was a member of the firm's Executive Committee. Jeff has extensive experience in dealing with workplace problems in the transportation, manufacturing, Internet, pharmaceutical, and health care industries. He has a bachelor's degree from the University of Pittsburgh and a law degree from the University of Pennsylvania.

What type of employment agreements should I make my employees sign before joining me?

There are several types of agreements that may be appropriate depending on the circumstances. Most employers find it useful to adopt agreements protecting their trade secrets or other confidential and proprietary information. In today's Information Age, the principal assets of many companies are not in plant and equipment but in knowledge. When the most valuable assets of the company go home every night with the employees, it is important to make sure those assets are not given away to competitors.

Employees who are in a position to develop new and useful products or applications may be able to take them elsewhere if the company does not have an employee invention agreement. This kind of agreement may not be appropriate for every employee, but it can be indispensable for some.

A third common agreement is one to protect an employer from competition during and after the time the employee works for the company. Noncompete agreements, which are sometimes called restrictive covenants, preclude the employee from working for a competing enterprise for a period of time. Usually, these agreements cover specific job duties, a particular geographic area, and a limited time frame.

Other common agreements include acknowledgments for receipt of the company's employee manual or specific personnel policies, such as a nondiscrimination policy or sexual harassment policy. These acknowledgments also commonly include the employee's agreement to read and comply with the policies. It is especially common to see employees acknowledge and agree that their employment will be at-will, meaning that either they or the employer can terminate the relationship at any time, with or without cause.

Will employee agreements hold up in a court of law?

It is hard to answer a question such as this in the abstract because the laws vary from state to state. Agreements that are routinely enforceable in one state might not be enforceable at all in another, or their enforcement might depend upon compliance with a series of technicalities.

As a general rule, most states will enforce confidentiality agreements, employee invention agreements, and agreements recognizing that the employment is at-will. Noncompete agreements are somewhat problematic because some states have a public policy that is hostile to them due to the anticompetitive impact they can have. Although you must always check the law of each state, as a general rule, most states will uphold noncompete agreements if they are narrowly tailored to meet a protectible business interest. What this is will vary depending on the unique circumstances of each case.

What exactly is a noncompete agreement?

A noncompete agreement is often a series of different commitments rolled into one document. Typical noncompete agreements include confidentiality provisions to protect the company's proprietary information, prohibit the employee from soliciting employees to work for a rival firm, preclude the employee from soliciting customers of the employer, and also bar the employee from owning or working for any company that is a business competitor of the employer. Each of these commitments could be handled in a separate document because each represents a separate undertaking, and some companies try to break them apart for various business reasons.

A confidentiality agreement is designed to protect the proprietary information of the employer. Confidentiality agreements typically go beyond trade secrets to protect a company's financial information, customer lists, vendor lists, the identity of employees, marketing plans, production processes, and similar information, even when they do not qualify as true trade secrets.

A nonsolicitation agreement usually comes in two forms. The first obligates an employee not to solicit any current employees to leave their employment to work for another entity. A variation of this also obligates the employee not to solicit employees, contractors, or vendors to terminate or reduce their business dealings with the company. The second type of nonsolicitation agreement is focused on customers. It obligates the employee either to agree not to solicit any customers on behalf of a rival company or not to solicit any customers that the employee dealt with during her employment. In some cases, a nonsolicitation-of-customers agreement can be similar in effect to a noncompete agreement.

A true noncompete agreement is broader than an agreement not to solicit customers. It typically prohibits the employee from engaging in any competition with the company for a stated period of time. Competition is not always easy to define. Is it only a company that is already in the same line of business? What about a company that is in a line of business that the first company is planning to enter? Noncompete agreements are usually drafted to deal with this kind of situation. Are two companies competitors if they are located in the same town? Perhaps, but not always. Some businesses are so local in their geographic reach that a distance of only a few miles is enough to eliminate any real competitive threat.

Noncompete agreements are also broader than nonsolicitation agreements in another important way. A nonsolicitation agreement protects against having a former employee call upon the customers of his former company. It does not prohibit the same person from starting a new company targeted to serving those same customers. That is why noncompete agreements typically prohibit the former employee from owning, accepting employment by, or performing services for a competitor. Such language effectively prohibits the employee from engaging in competition in the guise of being an independent contractor rather than an employee of the new company.

Would I be better with a nonsolicit clause, which would prevent employees from going after my customers/clients?

It depends on many factors. What is the nature of the employee's duties? Can the employee effectively cause damage in other ways? What is the nature of the company's relationship with its customers? In other words, how long will it take to hire and train a replacement, introduce that replacement to the customer, and allow the replacement to demonstrate sufficient competence to avoid "unfair" competition. Each situation is unique. While a noncompete agreement would obviously be more complete in protecting a company's interest, it may not always be available because local law may not look favorably on the anticompetitive aspects of such an obligation. Some states will enforce a nonsolicit clause for longer periods of time than they will enforce a broader agreement not to compete. A company must consider what it really needs to protect itself and balance the advantages and disadvantages of each approach given its unique circumstances.

Can a client contact an employee who has left and ask him to do work and would that invalidate the noncompete or nonsolicit agreement he signed with me?

Again, the answer depends on a variety of factors. If the employee signed a binding noncompete agreement, it should not matter whether the employee contacted the customer or the customer contacted the employee. The employee is still in competition. If the employee signed a nonsolicitation agreement, you will have to look further. Under local law, does *solicit* mean that the employee must be the actor? If so, then there will be a serious proof problem for the employer. It will be extremely difficult to prove that the employee solicited the customer, rather than the other way around. On the other hand, if the nonsolicitation agreement is worded to include any efforts by the employee to induce customers to do business, then it should not matter if the client asked the employee to do work. The agreement, by its terms, would bar the employee from doing so.

Does each state have different laws regarding noncompetes?

Absolutely. In addition, it is not always easy to know which state's law applies. Suppose a sales representative lives in New Jersey, but calls on accounts in Pennsylvania, New Jersey, and New York for a company based in California. Which state law will govern? Will one state's law govern the confidentiality agreement provisions and another state's law govern the noncompete provisions? The answer can depend on a variety of issues, including the state in which someone first files suit.

What if the employee invented a product or service while she was working for me, but it was done off-site?

In the absence of an agreement, an employee will generally retain the right to these inventions, but there are exceptions to the rule. The answers may turn on the following questions: Was the invention the thing the employee had been hired to develop? Does the invention involve creation or use of a trade secret of the employer? Is the inventor an officer of the company or someone who may have an implied duty to turn the information about the invention over to the company? Were any company facilities or personnel involved in reducing the invention to practice? Can the invention be patented?

Because of the complexity of results and the value of certainty, it is wise to have each employee sign an agreement that spells out rights to any invention during the term of the employee's work for the company.

If the employee leaves and six months later he announces a product whose idea could have come from his work at my company, do I have a claim?

Inventions developed after termination of employment generally belong to the employee unless the invention is derived from the employer's trade secrets or there is a valid contract requiring disclosure and assignment of the postemployment invention to the employer. Such postemployment invention agreements are sometimes treated as postemployment restrictive covenants. Thus care must be taken with their use.

In all of these cases, however, there will always be the question of when the moment of invention occurred. If the invention was conceived of during employment and reduced to practice after the employment ended, depending on the contractual or other understandings of the parties, the employer may have some rights to the invention. To avoid these problems, it is good practice to have an agreement that provides for the disclosure of inventions and discoveries conceived during the employment and to provide for their assignment to the employer. Sometimes these agreements also cover inventions that are reduced to practice within six months or a year after the employment ends, regardless of when they were conceived. Longer periods of time are often struck down as excessive restrictive covenants.

What is a trade secret?

Under the Uniform Trade Secrets Act, which has been adopted in some form by more than 40 states, a trade secret is typically defined as information, including a formula, pattern, compilation, program, device, method, technique or process, that:

1. Derives independent economic value, actual or potential, from not being generally known to, and not being readily ascertainable by proper means by, other persons who can obtain economic value from its disclosure or use, and
2. Is the subject of efforts that are reasonable under the circumstances to maintain its secrecy.

Trade secrets should be distinguished from secrets of the trade. For example, while most people in the country do not know how to interface a server with the worldwide web, this skill is a secret of the trade of being an Internet service provider. It is not a trade secret since almost all people in the trade already know it. On the other hand, a computer program used to manage inventory and process e-commerce procurement functions could be a trade secret if the company takes appropriate steps to protect its secrecy.

How does it relate to an Internet content, e-commerce, or Internet application?

As with any new technology, there is a process by which the established intellectual property laws must come to accommodate the unique problems that are created. The trade secret law has been drafted in functional ways that allow it to meet this challenge without much of a hiccup.

As a general rule, once content reaches the Internet, it will likely lose its status as a trade secret because it will become generally known. As one court noted, Internet postings should be treated in the same manner as if the information had been published in more traditional ways such as via newspaper or magazine. At the same time, there is an enormous possibility of mischief that can be created if Internet users can utilize anonymous remailers to protect their identity while they are in the process of destroying valuable intellectual property rights by posting them on the Internet.

As courts continue to grapple with these problems, we can expect them to take a discerning look at the circumstances surrounding the posting of trade secrets on the Internet. While courts will no doubt work to protect the rights of innocent third parties who acquire information off the Internet, they will have to balance this against the rights of the trade secret owner. This may not be easy given First Amendment principles concerning prior restraints on free speech. In one celebrated case, a court refused to issue a preliminary injunction to prohibit the threatened posting of Ford Motor Company's trade secrets on the Internet. Of course, this would not prohibit the trade secret owner from suing for damages, but such relief may come too late and be of no value if the defendant is judgment proof.

For how long is a trade secret protected?

Potentially forever. Just ask the people who guard the secret formula for Coca-Cola. Unlike a patent or copyright, each of which has a limited lifetime of legal protection, a trade secret can continue indefinitely. The test is whether it remains a trade secret (i.e., is it still of economic value and not generally known to or ascertainable by others who could obtain value from it?).

Do I have to have a special agreement that covers trade secrets or should it be included in employment agreements?

One benefit of establishing something as a trade secret is that it will be entitled to legal protection even in the absence of an employment agreement. Not only are employees at risk of liability if they disclose a trade secret, but in some states, the "inevitable disclosure" doctrine can be used to prohibit them from taking jobs with new employers in which they will inevitably utilize their former employer's trade secrets in doing the new job.

A business would not be wise to rely on this protection, however, because it is not easy to meet the trade secret threshold. The advantage of having an employment agreement covering confidentiality or imposing a noncompete obligation is that the employer can get extra protection. Even if information is not a trade secret, it may still be proprietary and subject to legal protection under a properly worded employment agreement. Even if an employee will not inevitably utilize trade secret data in a new job, a narrowly written noncompete agreement can prevent the employee from working for a competitor for a reasonable period of time.

What is a restrictive covenant?

Restrictive covenant is another term for a noncompete agreement. Basically, it is a covenant in an agreement that restricts the activities of the employee following the end of the employment relationship.

Whom does it apply to?

A restrictive covenant is most frequently found in employment contracts. It can, however, also be used in connection with the hiring of consultants who could cause business injuries if they then consulted for rival firms or used the information they gained from the consulting experience to compete against their former client. Restrictive covenant agreements are also commonly found in agreements to sell a business. Typically, the owners and officers of the selling company agree that they will not compete against the buyer for a period of time after the sale.

How does it relate to an Internet business?

Although the Internet may be a recent technology and a growing force in the world of commerce, it remains a business like any other. Indeed, because the worth of an Internet business consists primarily of intellectual property, the value of a restrictive covenant is greater here than in old-economy enterprises. Someone with inside knowledge of how to operate an oil refinery would need tens of millions of dollars to get a foothold, but a few thousand dollars is enough to enable an entrepreneur to launch a successful Internet business. With such low barriers to entry, it becomes more important than ever for employers to protect themselves against unfair competition from their former employees or consultants.

CHAPTER SUMMARY

Investors and future employees like to know that their money and careers are in the hands of smart people. There are three things you should never worry about when building a company:

- *Losing your job.* If you can hire people who are better and smarter than you and they can make your stock worth more than if you ran the company yourself, do so. It is your obligation and duty to yourself, your shareholders, and your employees to give the company the best chance of succeeding.

- *Negative response from big names.* If you believe the president of a Fortune 500 company would be the ideal chairman/CEO or that the head of marketing for one of the e-commerce leaders is just the person you need to make the company a success, don't hesitate to contact her. How many times have you thought about asking the prettiest girl in the room—who is standing by herself—to dance, but were afraid she would turn you down, only to watch a very average-looking guy get her? If you don't have the guts to go after the best, what does that say about the future of your company?

- *Giving up control.* No one person, especially in an e-commerce business, has the skills and knowledge to build a fast-growing company by micromanaging the process. Find people who are willing to take responsibility and give it to them.

Finally, great headhunters can help you get a higher valuation because of the level of professionals they have contact with. The formula for attracting money is

Great Management + Great Business Model = Investment

6

ATTRACTING, MANAGING, AND RETAINING EMPLOYEES

Every entrepreneur who starts a company usually goes to friends and family when putting together a management team. My first piece of advice when putting together a team is to stay away from family and only hire close friends you have worked with in the past. Never hire family because more than likely you will have to fire them for lack of performance or because the job has outgrown the family member's capabilities.

A past mentor of mine once hired his father-in-law at the suggestion of his wife. The father had good big-corporation experience, but couldn't adjust to an entrepreneurial business. The husband told the father-in-law that it wasn't working and a change had to be made. My mentor said their marriage was never the same and he ended up divorcing his wife.

A client of mine went into business with a lifelong friend whom he had never worked with. The two men had different styles. Eventually the partnership and friendship broke up. One day I ran into the ex-partner at a restaurant and told him I was having lunch with John, his former partner, and he told his companion that he couldn't eat in the same building as John and left.

One of the most successful entrepreneurs in the Philadelphia area hired three of his brothers to work for him. Over time, he ended up falling out with all three. To this day, none of the brothers speak with him.

SIX SOURCES FOR FINDING QUALITY EMPLOYEES

The following six excellent sources for finding quality managers won't cost you anything:

1. *Accountants.* Accountants usually have clients who are laying off people or selling a business. Sometimes the accountant is contacted by individuals looking for positions. Professionals send accountants resumes because they know accountants have clients who may be looking for people. The large national accounting firms such as BDO Seidman *(www.bdo.com)*, KPMG International *(www.kpmg.com)*, Deloitte & Touche *(www.dttus.com)*, PricewaterhouseCoopers *(www.pwcglobal.com)*, and Ernst & Young *(www.ey.com)* have internal recruiters who place exclients and friends of the firm with entrepreneurial companies.

2. *Attorneys.* Like accountants, attorneys have strong, far-reaching networks of contacts. They receive a lot of resumes and are glad to make contacts for people because it strengthens their relationships with clients.

3. *Economic development authorities.* Every county in the United States, every province in every country in Europe, and every country around the world has an economic development organization whose job is to lure companies to their locale. Many of these organizations—such as the Council for Urban Economic Development *(www.cued.org)* and the American Economic Development Council *(www.aedc.org)*—keep databases of individuals looking for new opportunities.

4. *Chambers of commerce.* Every good-sized town around the world has a chamber of commerce. Chambers usually have a database of individuals looking for positions and/or have a website with a section that advertises opportunities among their members. Membership service professionals in chambers have tremendous contacts and are good at identifying potential employees. A great comprehensive list of chambers of commerce nationally and internationally can be found at *www.chamberofcommerce.com.*

5. *Trade associations.* If you are looking for a specific type of professional, you can go to the trade association your website is marketing to. If

you don't know the association's name or if you want to know if there are multiple associations that focus on your market, go to the Association for Association Executives *(www.asaenet.org/main)*. The best associations in which to find Internet-focused professionals are Internet Business Alliance *(www.ibaonline.com)*, Internet Advertising Bureau *(www.iab.net)*, Association of Interactive Media *(www.interactivehq.org)*, and Information Industry Technology Council *(www.itic.org)*.

6. *Online recruiting.* A number of online recruiting sites have many quality resumes, but every in-house recruiting group will be competing with you to snap up these employees. In a startup, it is better to network your region and the industry you are focusing on than to go to these sites. If you want to cover all the bases, go to Monster Board *(www.monster.com)*, Headhunter *(www.headhunter.net)*, and Job Village *(www.jobvillage.com)*.

ATTRACTING EMPLOYEES

After working with dozens of Internet startups, I've learned the profile of the type of professional who is attracted to work in an Internet enterprise. He

- Is typically, but not always, a college graduate, although the ones who aren't just didn't want to go to or finish college.
- Is a creative problem solver.
- Is highly motivated and willing to work long hours.
- Needs to have input on what he is asked to do.
- Needs some degree of autonomy.
- Wants to work for smart people.
- Wants to be intellectually challenged.
- Thinks that cash compensation is important, but stock options are more important.

Your managers have to be smart and secure because if they aren't, you won't be able to attract the best people. Although the dot.com world is going through a shakeout of sorts, if you read *Venture Wire (www. venturewire.com)*, you will see lists of thousands of companies during the course of a year that have received private and institutional funding, and all of them are after the same people.

FOUR KEYS TO MOTIVATING EMPLOYEES

Running an Internet company isn't like coaching a football team or running a manufacturing company where people have to do basic things correctly, don't ask a lot of questions, and do what they are told. The companies that are most successful in motivating employees offer the following:

1. *Opportunity to fail.* Many leaders are risk-averse so their companies simply limp along. They can't attract the best, because smart, ambitious people want to push the envelope. Employees can't be afraid that they will lose their jobs if they try something and fail. Failure in the short term is like putting a deposit in a savings account. Eventually those deposits of experience will add up, and you will have developed a seasoned and effective employee.

2. *Responsibility and authority.* Individuals who work in an Internet company thrive on challenge. They want to be held accountable for projects they are involved in, but at the same time they want the authority to decide what is best. You can't micromanage people in this industry. They feel stifled and will leave, regardless of their cash compensation.

3. *Company recognition.* Everyone likes to be recognized for the good work that they do, especially people who work in the Internet. They consider themselves to be artists, creative problem solvers, and visionaries, and they want to be applauded and stroked when they do something well. Companies that establish monthly award programs that include certificates along with cash bonuses, free dinners, or weekend jaunts will create loyalty and spur everyone to work even harder. Just putting someone's name on a plaque like you see at a fast-food restaurant will do more harm

than good. The employees need something tangible. I have given away free dinners and overnight stays in hotels, because the award winners can report back to the group that they used and enjoyed the award.

4. *Financial recognition.* If you haven't worked in an entrepreneurial company in the past and the places that have employed you gave stock options out only to managers, then you need to readjust your thinking. Entrepreneurial companies typically can't pay as much in cash or do not have the stability of existing profitable companies, so everyone has to receive stock options. Employees who feel like owners will put in more time at the office and outside the office, too. Set up bonus structures for reaching certain internal development, sales, marketing, and cost-saving goals.

TEN TACTICS FOR RETAINING EMPLOYEES

Although this is a book about how to start and finance an e-commerce company, you'd better give a lot of thought to how you are going to keep the talent you recruit. Retaining employees is probably more important that recruiting new ones. You want to make sure that customers, investors, and new recruits view the company as stable and growing.

When I interviewed 30 CEOs for a newspaper column, their biggest concern was how to keep people from defecting to other companies. Here are 10 tactics you should employ to retain employees as soon as the first employee comes aboard:

1. *Sustenance.* You are probably laughing about this, but in the technology and Internet world where employees typically work 12 to 14 hours a day, it is imperative that you provide snacks and drinks during the day and dinner at night. One of my client's chief financial officers thought up the brilliant idea of letting employees order dinner at night and subtracting it from their paychecks at the end of each quarter. When employees heard this idea was being considered, they brought out the rope to string up the CFO and prepared their resumes to send to friends and recruiters. The CEO had to send out an e-mail saying the rumor was a bad joke.

2. *Employee recruiting.* Many companies ask the human resource department to run an advertisement for a position that needs to be filled. The HR person will interview candidates and introduce the best to the manager the person will be working for. Then the manager will make a selection. Entrepreneurial companies require acceptance from the employees because the company is small and people have to jell for the organization to grow and be successful. It is important in the early stages of a company's life to allow as many people as possible to be involved with the interview process. In the ventures I run, I don't hire anyone unless everyone is in agreement. By doing this, new people know they don't have to prove to anyone that they belong.

3. *Games.* The best ways for employees to unwind is through non-computer games. Many companies have set up game rooms or have partnered with other companies in their buildings to develop a game room. The game rooms have pool, Ping-Pong, and Foosball tables. In one of the companies I ran, I allowed the developers to create an online football pool where betting couldn't surpass a dollar per week. You can also set up fitness gyms.

4. *Raises.* Don't wait for your people to ask you for a raise. Purchase regional salary surveys and give raises appropriately or increase nontaxable fringe benefits. The raises don't have to be implemented at one time. Nor do they have to be all in cash. You can spread payments out and/or offer additional stock options. I have made it a practice to try to stay ahead of the salary curve, even if I couldn't financially afford to do it. I would call the employee in and tell her I was raising her pay, but it wouldn't begin until a certain date, or I would tell her we were accruing it and would pay the additional sum at the end of the quarter. Going to employees before they come to you builds loyalty and trust.

5. *Vacation.* Most entrepreneurs hate the thought of their employees taking vacation so they typically limit vacation to two weeks the first year and three weeks after five years. It has been my experience that you should encourage employees to take vacations and that you should allow them to earn extra days when they put in additional hours. Most employ-

ees of entrepreneurial companies have to be forced to take vacations because they are so focused on what they are doing. You need to encourage and possibly force people to take vacations so they won't burn out.

6. *Training.* Smart people want to acquire new skills. Develop a training budget and also ask vendors to run luncheon training sessions that brief employees about new technology, marketing, and sales strategies. Vendors love to do this and are willing to pay for lunch for everyone who attends.

7. *Reading.* Encourage people to read a variety of magazines and books. I had a client that budgeted $100 per employee per year to buy whatever business books and magazines they wanted.

8. *Sick leave.* If someone isn't feeling well, insist that he go home, rest, and come back when he feels well enough. Don't make employees feel that it is a weakness to call in sick or that they are letting their peers down. The last thing you need is everyone catching what one person has. Also, facilitating sick leave shows you put people before the business.

9. *Children.* If an employee's child has a play, ball game, or something else special, insist that the employee be with the child. You want employees to know that family comes before business and you don't want them to be mentally distracted because they are regretting not going to their child's game. Even more important is letting employees work at home when a child is sick.

10. *Mentors.* Everyone needs someone to bounce ideas off, provide advice, and discuss concerns with. Developing a mentorship program helps employees grow professionally. In the beginning, when you have only a few people, ask your board members or business associates if they would be willing to mentor someone. Most people consider it a high compliment to mentor someone.

At the end of the day, your success is dependent on having happy, fulfilled employees. Don't take them for granted.

CHAPTER SUMMARY

I can't stress enough the importance of recruiting the best people. Attracting great people will attract both investors and other talented people. To find the best people, remember to use the following sources:

- Accountants
- Attorneys
- Economic development professionals
- Chambers of commerce
- Trade associations
- Online recruiting

Don't settle for anything but the best. Investors will judge you by the type of people you recruit. Remember, investors are not just investing in you and your business model; they are also betting on the team you put together. Finally, work as hard to make your employees happy as you do your customers.

7

How to Pick
Quality Service Providers

There are two teams that investors evaluate when deciding whether they will invest in a company. One is the entrepreneur's internal management team. The second team is the outside consultants he hires that provide business planning, legal, accounting, insurance, and financing advice. The outside consultants you hire will say as much about your company as the people you hire on your internal team.

Most people just take a friend's referral, call someone in an advertisement, or hire someone they met at an event. Selecting someone that management met through a referral or event is a good way to get started, but should not be the full extent of a service provider search. Selecting the wrong type of outside professionals can cost the company money and credibility in the investment community. Management needs to be selective and thorough in its evaluation and choice of key outside professionals.

EVALUATING SERVICE PROVIDERS

There are 10 questions to ask when hiring outside professionals:

1. Do they have experience at working with Internet companies?
2. How many years have they been in the business?

3. Have they ever worked with a startup e-commerce company?

4. Are their fees reasonable?

5. Will they work with us financially if we can't afford their full fees in the beginning?

6. What do their clients say about them?

7. When clients have left them, what were the reasons?

8. Can they grow with our business?

9. Will a seasoned executive be assigned to us or will we be used to allow a junior executive to get some experience?

10. Will they introduce us to financing sources and their other clients who can potentially bring us business?

Most companies need four types of professionals: an accountant, a banker, an insurance broker, and a lawyer. Let's discuss each of these questions and how they relate to hiring outside professionals.

1. Do they have experience at working with Internet companies?

All too often, businesspeople hire outside professionals based on personality or a friend's recommendation. They hire an accountant because they hear she is meticulous and got tax money back for a friend. Another friend said this lawyer was terrific at helping him incorporate. The insurance broker got them a lower premium on their car insurance. The banker was helpful in getting a friend an increase on his line of credit.

Those kinds of references are a good start, but what management really needs to know is whether the professionals have ever worked with an Internet-related business. Do they understand how much money it takes to be successful on a national or international basis? Do they have contacts that can cut the time it takes to get to profitability?

Example:

Accountant: Internet companies need accountants who are familiar with state, regional, and national tax issues. One of my clients sells handmade products from European artisans on his website. He needs an accounting firm that can set up an accounting system that tracks sales by country and by state. This is important so he can make sure that he pays the appropriate taxing bodies.

2. How many years have they been in the business?

Experience is very important to any business, but it could mean the difference between success and failure in a startup. Management wants professionals who have been around long enough to have personally experienced the unavoidable ups and downs of business. Management should look at professionals with 10 to 15 years of experience because these people have gone through ups and downs and have learned most of the tricks of their trade.

Example:

Accountant: An experienced accountant will know what hidden expenses to look for that can be eliminated or provide additional deductions. A national accounting firm or a regional accounting firm with an entrepreneurial practice will give investors confidence that experienced advice on handling tax issues and reducing burn rate (cash being spent by the business) is being implemented appropriately.

3. Have they ever worked with a startup e-commerce company?

Any manager who has been in involved in a distressed company knows the psychological and financial issues management has to deal with. Management needs professionals who are calm and experienced at advising and servicing troubled companies.

Example:

Banker: Management wants a banker that will help them leverage investor cash and develop a loan package based on cash flow instead of company profits.

4. Are their fees reasonable?

Management shouldn't be shy about asking about a service provider's fees up-front. Make sure the charges are comparable to what others charge in the company's geographic area.

Example:

Lawyers: If you are raising money from local private investors, you will need a regional law firm with venture capital and Internet client experience. If you are raising money from venture capitalists, you will need a prestigious national law firm such as Morrison & Forester. Most corporate attorneys at small regional firms were either with large regional or national firms or else with medium or large companies. Their fees, in most cases, are half that of a large firm.

5. Will they work with us financially if we can't afford their full fees in the beginning?

If management does a good job of selling itself, the company, and the e-commerce focus of the company, most professionals will work out suitable payment arrangements.

Examples:

Accountants: Accounting firms have flexibility because they charge for their time. These professionals always budget for a certain amount of low- or no-fee time for companies they believe have potential. A friend of mine started an online exchange to sell work clothes and was trying to raise capital. He went to a big accounting firm and made a presentation to a couple of the partners. They were so impressed with his experience, attention to detail, and plan for developing the company that they agreed to provide $10,000 worth of free services until he raised the money. They even offered to introduce him to private investors.

Lawyers: Like accounting firms, lawyers can provide flexible payment terms. There are firms that have taken stock and warrants in lieu of their fees or to make up for unpaid fees. A friend of mine used a big law firm to close a deal with a venture fund. The lawyer involved had worked many years with the venture community and entrepreneurial companies. He liked the deal and agreed to waive his up-front fees; he assigned a junior lawyer to handle the uncomplicated parts of the transaction. My friend received top-flight, big-name support for the cost of a lesser-known attorney and firm.

6. *What do their clients say about them?*

Ask service providers for references. Contact those references to make sure the service providers live up to their billing. Ask other service providers to recommend professionals outside of their field. Ask an accountant to recommend a lawyer and vice versa. Professional service providers have experience working with each other and they don't want to make a bad recommendation. The best groups to ask for referrals are private investor groups, venture capital trade associations, and venture funds.

7. *When clients have left them, what were the reasons?*

Always try to find and speak with the clients who have left service providers that you are considering. There are many reasons clients leave, and a lot of them don't have anything to do with performance. Personalities and the ways of doing business may not have matched.

8. *Can they grow with our business?*

If management is trying to grow a business larger than a couple of million in sales and possibly go international, the company will need a firm that has experience in larger businesses and has an international department or affiliations with other firms around the world. The company doesn't have to be a large company to consider selling abroad.

Example:

Bankers: Ask the bank's management what its lending limit is; the answer will give you an idea of the size of companies it can handle. Most small regional banks have lending limits under $5 million. If that is a consideration, you need to develop a relationship with a large regional bank.

9. Will a seasoned executive be assigned to us or will we be used to allow a junior executive to get some experience?

Most firms of any size will assign a partner to handle complex issues and an associate to handle the smaller issues. Many times the associates will have developed an area of expertise that the partner doesn't have and can be more valuable. It is important to know that an experienced executive who has handled problems such as the ones management is facing will be available. If management wants to know about the level of service, look at service providers' business cards to see if they give the home telephone, pager, and car phone numbers. If so, you know they provide superior service in terms of round-the-clock availability. This has been my observation and experience.

> *Example:*
>
> *Accountants:* Partners of accounting firms will assign junior people to audits, but will work with the client on personal and corporate tax strategies that determine the company's corporate structure. There is an accountant in Philadelphia who works for one of the large international firms. He is at the top of every startup company's list because he is known to be available to his clients 24 hours a day, seven days a week, and he has a wealth of experience. Presidents of companies like to brag about how they had a problem and this person was willing to discuss it on a Saturday night and how he could provide solutions to complex problems based on his experiences with other clients.

10. Will they introduce us to financing sources, such as their other clients, who can potentially bring us business?

All good service professionals should have a diverse and large database of contacts. Such a contact source is an extra value that they can provide. If all else between professionals under consideration is equal, management chooses the one who can open doors for new business and can provide advice and capital.

There are banks, accounting firms, and law firms that hold seminars for their clients on a wide range of topics and bring in other service providers who are expert in fields they know little about. These seminars usually attract potential new business.

WHO IS THE MOST IMPORTANT SERVICE PROVIDER?

The most important service provider you will hire as a startup is your attorney. Experienced venture attorneys know what should be in a term sheet, how to negotiate a fair deal, and how not to kill a deal, and they have strong venture capital contacts. The following interview with one of the country's leading venture capital attorneys concerns how to select attorneys and what value they bring.

John F. Delaney is a partner in the New York office of Morrison & Forester, where he serves as co-chair of the office's New Media Practice Group. His clients include some of the Internet industry's best-known companies, including Yahoo!, EarthWeb, Razorfish, Office.com, and uBid. Born in Anchorage, Alaska, John received his BA from the University of Notre Dame in 1986, graduating with honors. In 1989, he received his JD from Columbia Law School, where he was an executive editor of The Journal of Law and the Arts. *John is a member of both the California Bar and the New York Bar.*

Should you select an attorney before you go after venture capital or after a venture capitalist expresses interest in investing?
That depends on the type of attorney and legal service that you are looking for. Given the huge demand that currently exists for high-quality attorneys in new media, a well-known or experienced lawyer or law firm may be reluctant to spend too much time working with you on your financing until a venture capitalist has expressed interest in investing, most commonly evidenced by a draft term sheet. [A term sheet is an offer by a venture capitalist detailing how much the venture capitalist wants to invest and what he wants in return for his investment.] The lawyer may be less reluctant if you agree to put up a retainer or otherwise convince her that she is not taking a substantial risk by devoting time and resources to a venture that has not been funded. Therefore, if you approach certain types of attorneys too early, you may not be successful in engaging them—which is ironic, since attorneys often encourage startups to seek legal counsel as early as possible. If you already have an attorney or law firm that performs your

company's day-to-day legal work, then that attorney or law firm should be able to shepherd you through at least the term sheet stage. However, if your current legal counsel is constrained by resources or does not have extensive experience in the new media space, you may want to "upgrade" legal counsel for the preparation of the transaction documents and negotiation and closing of the deal. In some cases, your new legal counsel may even be able to work with your current legal counsel.

However, once you have a draft term sheet from a venture capitalist, the "top-tier" venture attorneys are likely to be more enthusiastic about representing you—particularly if the term sheet is from a prestigious or well-respected venture capitalist.

The most important thing to remember is never to sign a term sheet from a venture capitalist until it has been reviewed by an attorney experienced in venture capital transactions. Seeking venture capital legal expertise after signing the term sheet is a big mistake—the term sheet may already bind you to horrendous and unfair terms, and once it is signed, even an experienced venture attorney will be constrained by what is in the term sheet.

If you hire a venture attorney, will he assist you in finding venture capital?

Although an attorney's primary job is to provide effective legal counsel, a good venture attorney, like any good service provider, should allow his client to benefit from the attorney's network of contacts. A well-connected venture attorney is no substitute for a well-thought-out business plan and an impressive management team. That being said, the fact that you are represented by a well-known venture lawyer will bring additional credibility to you and your company when you meet with a venture capitalist—even if your lawyer did not personally arrange the meeting. Investors like to know that the companies they are investing in have top-tier legal representation.

A good venture lawyer can provide you with valuable insights about the venture capital community (which is even more important than arranging introductions). For example, if your business plan focuses on the financial services community, your lawyer may know what venture funds are interested in the financial services market. Similarly, your lawyer may be able to save you a lot of time and effort by steering you away from venture funds that have a poor reputation or are known not to invest in companies that share your company's focus.

Should you hire a local venture attorney if the venture capitalist is local?

Thanks to e-mail, cell phones, video conferencing, and other electronic communications tools, it is no longer essential for your venture capitalist and your attorney to be located in the same city. Indeed, your attorney no longer needs to be located in the same city as your company! Venture capitalists are used to dealing with law firms that are located in other cities, and most likely will not demand that your law firm be located in the same city as the venture fund. Rather, a venture capitalist will be much more interested in making certain that your law firm is experienced with venture capital financings—an inexperienced lawyer may slow down the deal, may waste time by dwelling on irrelevant issues or fighting for bizarre, atypical contract provisions, and may undermine the venture capitalist's confidence in your company as a whole (e.g., if this company is using an inappropriate attorney for its venture financing round, does that mean that the company's other legal matters have been handled in an incompetent manner? Should I be investing in this company?).

If all or part of the deal is being governed by the laws of a jurisdiction with unique rules, then you should make sure that your out-of-town attorney is familiar with those rules (or make sure that local co-counsel is retained) and that your out-of-town counsel is legally licensed and competent to render advice to you. For example, a California attorney may not be familiar with the rules of corporate governance for a company incorporated under New York laws, and a New York attorney might not be familiar with California's rules on noncompetition agreements. Also, if retaining an out-of-town attorney will mean additional travel and other costs, you should have an agreement beforehand as to who will bear those costs.

What types of fees are involved?

Most lawyers working in the venture capital area will bill your company on an hourly basis. Increasingly, venture lawyers are willing to defer billing until completion of the venture round, with the understanding that, if the round for some reason is never completed, your legal bills will still have to be paid. Also, many venture lawyers are willing to take a small equity stake in your company in return for a lower billing rate or a "cap" on legal fees; however, if your lawyer proposes this, you should consider retaining another lawyer to review the terms of the proposed equity stake.

What is the attorney's role in the deal?

Your attorney should let you know what to expect before you enter into negotiations (the most common misconception on the part of entrepreneurs is that papering the deal is a very simple process), educate you about the law and market norms so that you can make informed decisions, and be proactive in shepherding the deal along to closing. Your attorney also has a responsibility to measure speed of closing against your best interests and be vocal about unreasonable deal points. An attorney who has represented you in the past or who has had an opportunity to perform due diligence on your company may also have suggestions as to any corporate "cleanup" activities that you might undertake to make your company more attractive to prospective investors and/or prevent delays when a financing deal is being negotiated.

What types of information are venture attorneys aware of that make a deal run smoother?

Having had a prior relationship with the venture capitalist and experience working on other deals, a venture capitalist's attorney may know his client's "breaking points"—where and how much a company should press. A venture capitalist's attorney may also be familiar with how the venture capitalist works best and most efficiently. For example, does the venture capitalist like to be consulted on all details or only the major points? Also, an experienced venture lawyer will be familiar with trends in the venture industry—the kind of terms that venture capitalists are giving to entrepreneurs these days, new provisions that are designed to protect an entrepreneur's interests, and so forth.

What is the attorney's role after the deal is done?

After the deal is done, the attorney should prepare and distribute the closing documents so that the parties have an easily accessible reference source when questions about the terms of the transaction arise. The attorney should also retain a complete set of signed documents for safekeeping. Assuming that the attorney will continue to counsel the company, she should also be mindful of any restrictions that the company has agreed to as part of the deal (e.g., limits as to the number of options that may be granted under a stock option plan, the investor's right to maintain his percentage ownership in the company) and make sure that those restrictions are incorporated into future decisions. Also, if there are any postclosing covenants (e.g., delivery of certain legal papers or certificates), the attorney should assist the company in fulfilling them. Finally, because most companies going through one venture round usually can expect a subsequent round, the attorney can help you begin preparing for the next round.

CHAPTER SUMMARY

Use the same standards for evaluating and employing service providers that you used in recruiting your employees. Go after the best and don't worry about the initial price tag. If your business opportunity holds a lot of promise, service providers will make their figures work into your budget and cash flow.

- *Accountants:* Contact the local chamber of commerce and business organizations and ask your attorney and banker. Find out who is auditing other e-commerce companies in your region.
- *Lawyers:* Contact the local bar association and ask who are the company's accountant and banker.
- *Bankers:* Because accountants deal with finances, they are a good source for recommending banks and bankers. Also, contact the regional office of the Small Business Administration and any entrepreneurial/business organizations in the region.
- *Other:* Insurance and real estate have become such commodity businesses, and companies use them so infrequently, there is little need to comment on them at length. In the case of insurance, try using the Internet to find a vendor. There are insurance companies that provide price quotes via the Web, and that will allow you to buy directly (without needing an insurance agent). In real estate, it is just a matter of finding the right location and negotiating an acceptable price.

If you are pressed for time and plan to delegate to someone on your staff the interviewing and retaining of various service providers, make sure you take the time to interview the attorney representing you. In a startup that is raising money, the attorney is the most important outside hire you will make.

8

THE VALUE AND SELECTION OF A BOARD OF DIRECTORS OR ADVISORS

There are so many Internet companies vying for investment capital that one of the few ways to separate one's venture from the rest of the crowd is to attract quality directors and advisory board members. If you take a look at the best companies, one of the common threads is that they recruit quality board members—not just well-known names, but professionals with experience, contacts, and capital to invest.

There are two types of boards. The one most people are familiar with is a board of directors. A board of directors has fiduciary responsibility to the shareholders of the corporation. The second type of board is a board of advisors. They have no fiduciary responsibility and serve at the pleasure of the owner of the business.

Every corporation must have a board of directors, but that board can be one person. That one person has both a fiduciary responsibility and the liabilities that go with it. When outsiders are added to the board of directors, the company needs to buy liability insurance for the officers and directors. Board members don't want to be financially responsible for anything that may go wrong that they can't control.

For a startup company that can't afford or doesn't want to spend the money on directors-and-officers liability insurance to support a board of directors, creating an advisory board is the next best thing. Advisory boards serve at the pleasure of the owner/president. The company can and should grant these people stock options and/or pay them a consulting fee for their time. If the company is providing options and/or paying them a consulting fee, they will give the company their best effort. Also, paying them a consulting fee will cause management to take their suggestions seriously.

All too often, presidents of companies like to load their boards of directors with cronies and sycophants. Naturally, management wants people it likes on the board. Management also wants people who will support them through bad times as well as good, but management shouldn't want the board to put management's needs before the business's.

Unfortunately, many presidents would prefer to keep their positions of power rather than do what is best for the business. They forget they have an obligation to their investors, employees, clients, and vendors.

When selecting or evaluating board members, use the same approach as you would when hiring new employees. Here are 10 questions management needs to ask itself when selecting and evaluating board members:

1. What types of skills, contacts, and experiences are missing among the management group that the board can fill?

2. How can these people help us grow the business?

3. What mix of people are we looking for?

4. Where can we find these people?

5. How big a board do we need?

6. Do they understand our business?

7. Can they invest or help us raise money if we need it?

8. Can they help us bring in new business?

9. Should all board members be good strategic thinkers?

10. Will board members support well-thought-out but risky ideas, or will they abandon and turn on management if the ideas fail?

Insight into the answers for each of these questions is based on experience of a variety of my clients, as follows:

1. What types of skills, contacts, and experiences are missing among my management group that the board can fill?

A board should be thought of as an extension of the management team. The company might need someone who has been through a turnaround. A board member should also be someone management can confide in when it doesn't know what to do.

Management may be looking to raise additional capital and need the guidance of a seasoned banker, investment banker, or chief financial officer. If management is pursuing government contracts or is focusing on a niche market, management probably wants a board member or two who has experience and contacts in that area.

The management needs to look at the board as a group that can fill holes in the management group and understands the company's industry.

2. How can these people help management grow the business?

Look at the company's board members and determine if they have the experience and knowledge to help the business grow over a 5-to-10–year period. Have they been through the ups and downs and do they know what it takes to be successful? Are they people with whom management feels comfortable discussing problems and who give honest answers?

3. What mix of people are we looking for?

Try to get a mix of young and older people on the board. The younger people may be more knowledgeable about technology and what motivates younger employees. Many of my clients share the opinion that younger executives embrace new ideas and change more than older executives do. The reason, according to one of my clients, is that younger executives want to make their mark.

Not everyone has to have 30 years of business experience to provide value. Many established companies would have liked to have had Bill

Gates, chairman/CEO of Microsoft, on their boards when he was in his early 30s because of his vision and understanding of the computer field and business in general. We all have met some very insightful 30-year-olds who have more and better experience than some 50-year-olds.

On the other hand, receiving sage advice is reassuring. The experienced executive will teach management that the road to success is long, that patience is needed, and that no one is immune to difficult times.

Many companies are just starting to add very successful women to their boards. Women tend to be more nurturing, better listeners, and more practical than men. They are also more used to juggling families and managing the home on top of handling their professional duties. They are good problem solvers, especially in crisis situations that require a velvet touch over an iron fist.

4. *Where can we find these people?*

Talk to your accountant, lawyer, and banker; they are people who generally have a wide network. They want to see the company succeed, so they are going to recommend good people. Contact professional venture capitalists and ask them for names.

Look in the business section of the local newspaper and talk to people in the trade associations and chambers of commerce the company belongs to. As management comes across good people, develop a database and add them to it.

Practically all of my clients' board members have come from the above-mentioned sources. In fact, my clients tell me that some of their closest business associates and mentors were people they got to know through having them on their boards.

5. *How big a board do we need?*

Small companies don't need more than six board members. In a small company, six or eight is a good number and you'll get a good mix of views. Once you grow larger, you may want a larger board that can be allocated effectively into committees. Many successful entrepreneurs will tell you that if you need to have an odd number of board members because you are worried about the board being split on important issues, then more than likely the company will fail because everyone won't be pulling in the same direction.

6. *Do they understand our business?*

Have they run an Internet company or does their company buy and sell products over the Internet? The board members don't necessarily have to be experts in the e-commerce niche you are after, but it is extremely important that board members of an e-commerce company understand, embrace, and believe in the future of the Internet.

7. *Can they invest or help us raise money if we need it?*

Not every board member has to be wealthy enough to invest, but having a few board members who can is very valuable. When banks and venture capitalists see that some of the board members are also investors, it gives them comfort and a willingness to put in their money. If board members who can afford to put in money won't, that sends a negative message.

All of my clients tell me they personally like to see every board member have some financial stake in the company, regardless of the size of their investment. It can't be trivial, but it doesn't have to be great. This heightens the board's interest in the company and sends the signal to institutional investors that the board members have confidence in the company.

8. *Can they help us bring in new business?*

This goes back to the value of having board members who understand and have worked in the company's industry. Board members can bring valuable contacts that can lead to sales. All of my clients believe that every board member should be thought of as another member of the sales force.

One of my clients, who runs an e-commerce company providing electricity to health care facilities, brought on the CEO of an international health care consulting firm. This individual sent a letter to all of his firm's

5,000 clients promoting my client's site. Within six months, venture capitalists couldn't throw enough money at my client.

9. Should all board members be good strategic thinkers?

Not every board member can be a good strategic thinker, just as not every board member can be good at sales or raising money. Having board members who know how to think strategically can be invaluable. Most people are myopic and don't see how the rest of the world connects with their business. Strategic thinkers see opportunities and partnerships that will create sales relationships and new product opportunities.

One of my clients, who runs an e-commerce company that provides request-for-proposal services to companies looking for contractors, bought into the idea of one of his board members to private label his service for publications. My client now has an exclusive contract with a national newspaper chain.

10. Will board members support well-thought-out but risky ideas, or will they abandon and turn on management if the ideas fail?

The last problem management needs to encounter is board members second-guessing whatever new ideas management wants to implement. This can be very destructive. The best way to avoid such problems is to brief each board member in writing and then discuss the idea with the board as a group. Invite discussion, build consensus, and move forward.

BUILDING AND UTILIZING A BOARD OF DIRECTORS

Dr. Thomas P. Gerrity is professor of management at the Wharton School of the University of Pennsylvania and was dean of the Wharton School from 1990 to 1999. He is one of the most experienced and sought-after board members in the world. Dr. Gerrity is the founder and was for 20 years chief executive officer of the Index Group, one of the world's leading consulting firms in business reengineering and information technology strategy. Prior to going to Wharton, he was president of CSC Consulting, the worldwide commercial professional services division of Computer Sciences Corporation and the parent of CSC Index. He currently serves on the boards of several corporations such CVS, one of the country's largest retail drugstore chains; Fannie Mae, which provides mortgages; Internet Capital Group, the world's largest business-to-business Internet investor; Investorforce, the leading online community for money managers; and Knight-Ridder, one of the world's largest newspaper chains. A Rhodes scholar in economics at Oxford University, Dr. Gerrity received his doctorate in management from the Sloan School of Management at the Massachusetts Institute of Technology (1970). He also earned his bachelor's (1963) and master's (1964) degrees in electrical engineering from MIT. Dr. Gerrity served on the Sloan School faculty between 1968 and 1972.

What are board member responsibilities?

A director is obligated first and foremost to the shareholders, but also must give consideration to other stakeholders: debt holders, employees, and customers. In a startup, the board members typically have more hands-on involvement. Because the management team is not fully developed, the board might be involved in strategy, recruiting people, raising capital, and developing new customers.

How can an entrepreneur get the most out of her board?

You have to involve them and ask for their help. Use them as a sounding board. Use them as trusted counselors and advisors. It can be lonely at the top; it's good to have board members you can turn to for help. You need to inform them and let them know your thinking.

What types of skills and experiences should an entrepreneur look for?

You look for a mix of skills from financing to organization building to marketing. Typically you want to have some board members who are current or past CEOs.

Should an entrepreneur put his lawyer and accountant on the board?

No! That confuses their obligations. They have a professional obligation to the company, and you do not want to get them into a conflict-of-interest position.

Should personal friends be put on the board?

Again, you will have conflicts of interest. Why is it important to have a personal friend on the board? Usually people do that because it is easy. I would stay focused on building a board based on competence and stature.

How should a young entrepreneur go about recruiting high-profile, experienced business leaders such as yourself?

Writing letters to people you don't know won't get you anywhere. You need to network, be introduced by the right people, and then meet the candidates face-to-face. You need to be candid, open, and straightforward, because that's what a board member would expect.

How should a board member be compensated?

In a startup or young company, it is typical for the outside directors to receive options plus perhaps the option to invest. Also reimburse them for travel. You don't have to pay a fee.

Should board members be expected to invest their own money?

I think it is a good idea, but to get the right director, I wouldn't make it a deal breaker.

Should board members be expected to assist in raising money?

In general, I don't think you should expect it. However, you might recruit a director who can help you raise money. Board members can typically provide useful introductions.

How many hours a month, a quarter, or a year should a board member provide?

The board members should participate in all scheduled meetings. I would say the board of a young company should meet every six to eight weeks. You don't want them meeting so much that it consumes too much of their time and yours, but meet often enough to keep them informed.

How often should I meet with board members individually?

It depends on the CEO. In a young company where the board has just come together, it's important for the CEO to get to know each director.

Also, outside of full board meetings, each director has individual advice and counsel you may wish to solicit.

CHAPTER SUMMARY

Don't underestimate the value of recruiting quality board members to your venture. If you can attract the right people, then money, customers, media coverage, and blue chip employees will want to jump on the bandwagon. Recruiting the right board members takes time, patience, and especially guts enough to approach people who seem unapproachable. The best way to find top-notch board members is to get introductions from the following types of professionals:

- Managing partners of law and accounting firms
- Business writers for national and regional publications
- Presidents of regional and national trade associations

No matter how big the target, everyone is honored when someone contacts him to be on the board of directors or advisory board of a company. Settling for undeserving and unqualified people will undermine your chances of attracting capital.

9

PRESENTING
TO INVESTORS

The most stressful part of starting a new venture, as any entrepreneur will tell you, is raising capital. Raising capital is the first critical juncture in the life cycle of a business. Unfortunately, you can't run a business without capital, so founders have to be involved in the fund-raising process.

Raising capital is no different from selling any other product or service. You have to do the following things well:

- Develop a business plan that grabs investors' attention.
- Develop a list of attributes potential investors should have.
- Develop a list of potential private investors.
- Develop a list of potential institutional investors based on the criteria you have put together for the ideal potential investor.
- Develop a list of questions investors are most likely to ask. Cut and paste the answers from your business plan under each question.
- Develop a simple-to-understand handout for investors to follow as they listen to your presentation.
- Review and commit to memory your business plan.
- Put together a group of people who either are investors or deal with investors (such as accountants, investment bankers, and lawyers) and ask them to critique your presentation.

- Perform due diligence on prospective investors before you meet with them. This means finding out what types of companies they have invested in and what they are looking to invest in. Understand their hot buttons. One of my clients read a white paper on the Internet that one of the partners of a venture fund we were pitching to had written about viral marketing, so my client made sure that certain words found in the white paper were put in strategic sections of his presentation. The venture capitalist termed the phrase "viral marketing," which means spreading the word around about a business through word of mouth.

- Ask the potential investor what she likes about your concept as soon as you sit down to start the meeting. Having investors affirm what they like about your business will set a positive tone and will help you to focus your presentation on what is important to them.

AVOIDING COMMON MISTAKES MADE BY ENTREPRENEURS

Over the past 13 years, I have sat through hundreds of presentations. The reason many entrepreneurs don't receive investment is that they do such a poor sales job with the investor. Here's some advice gleaned from my observations.

1. *Provide good handouts.* Every handout should be simple to follow and have a lot of bulleted items to support your verbal presentation. Having no handout forces investors to take a lot of notes and then recall the significance of notes they have written and in what context they were written. When you meet institutional venture capitalists from companies such as Safeguard Scientifics and Benchmark, you must remember that you are one of five to eight presenters they are listening to that particular day, one of 30 to 40 that week, and one of 500 to 1,000 they listen to during the course of a year. You need to make their job easy.

2. *Stay focused.* Remember that you are like an entertainer on a stage and you are leading the audience. If you move from topic to topic and the topics don't appear to connect and the listener looks confused,

then you have a big problem. I once had a client who started his presentation by telling the prospective investor what deals they were working on and then shifted to their experience and then back to the deals they were working on. The investor was so confused that he asked the entrepreneur at the end of the session what exactly their business did. This was catastrophic because the prospective investor started the meeting by telling the entrepreneur he was very impressed with the business plan and thought it would make a great investment.

3. *Know your financials.* Nothing causes a prospective investor to lose confidence more quickly than watching the entrepreneur fumble through the financials or ask the trusted consultant brought to the presentation to answer the question. This actually happened to me a few times. We were presenting to a well-respected venture fund and my client turned to me and asked me to answer the venture capitalist's question because I had created the financials. The venture capitalist turned to the entrepreneur before I could answer and said that if I answered the question, the entrepreneur should leave the room so he could speak to me about the investment. Needless to say, the entrepreneur didn't get the fund's money.

4. *Bring knowledgeable teammates.* It is always a good idea to bring some of your key management with you when meeting with investors because the investors aren't investing just in you but in your team as well. The worst thing you can do is bring an uninformed new team member to an investor meeting and watch him flounder as he tries to answer questions whose answers he doesn't know. One of my clients was meeting a venture fund for the first time and the fund was very interested in investing. The client brought its new chief financial officer, who had been with the company for only a week. The client neglected to mention to the venture capitalists that the CFO had only recently come on board and then asked the CFO to answer certain financial questions. The CFO stumbled through the presentation, and the venture capitalists cut the meeting off early.

5. *No tales.* If you don't know the answer, tell the investors you don't know and you will get back to them. Venture capitalists see so many deals that they probably know the answer to the question they are asking you, so if you fake your answer, you kill your chances of getting an involvement.

6. *Use pictures.* If you are raising money for a product company, you should show through graphics how the product works and who will use it. One of my clients was an application service provider, and when we met with venture capitalists, she tried to describe the product and its uses verbally. No matter how many different examples the client gave, the venture capitalist was still not sure what the product did. The venture capitalist eventually got up and started to draw on a blackboard to see if he understood what the entrepreneur was telling him.

7. *Don't deny there's competition.* Every business has competition, yet many entrepreneurs will tell prospective investors that they don't have any competition. All venture capitalists and private investors I have ever dealt with roll their eyes when they hear an entrepreneur claim there's no competition. Entrepreneurs have to remember there is direct and indirect competition. An entrepreneur claiming to have no competition makes himself look naïve and insults the intelligence of prospective investors.

8. *Know your financial needs.* If the venture capitalists like what you have to say, then they will ask you how much money you want, how much you are valuing the company for, and how you will spend the money. I have been in presentations where the entrepreneurs did an exceptional job of explaining their product/service, but were vague on the amount of money they needed and how they would use it. The investors were left with the impression that the entrepreneurs knew their business, but weren't good businesspeople and hadn't identified someone with that skill. Not knowing your financial needs isn't a deal killer, but it can certainly delay a deal.

9. *Avoid unrealistic/unsubstantiated valuation.* A great presentation can be torpedoed by a valuation that isn't comparable to what others in the market are getting. For example, I had a client who was developing a very focused e-commerce site. He had no clients and his team was above average but not stellar. He had a good technology and first-mover advantage. When the VCs asked him how much he wanted and at what price, his response was so out of the realm of reality coupled with a poor response on how he arrived at his price that the VCs politely thanked him and walked away. Make sure you know what other companies are getting by reading *www.venturewire.com* and speaking

with valuation companies and accounting firms who work with companies like yours.

10. *Understand investors' motives and interest.* Never go into a presentation with potential investors without knowing and practicing the answers to the most likely questions you will be asked. It's much like preparing for a case before a judge and jury. Great lawyers never ask questions they can't answer. As I mentioned in the preceding paragraphs, one of the biggest mistakes you can make is not being prepared. If there is a question that you hadn't prepared for and you don't know the answer, tell the person asking the question you will call her back with the answer.

RAISING CAPITAL

I interviewed Rob Weber, who has been working with entrepreneurial companies for almost two decades. He has directly and indirectly raised over $30 million for the companies he has worked for and has financed out of his own pocket. Recently, he raised over $4 million for an Internet customer service application company called Knoa.

Rob Weber is president of Weber Associates, a strategic marketing and financing firm serving high-technology growth businesses. He started his career in venture capital, providing seed capital and strategic planning support to emerging growth companies, with the investment banking firm of Howard, Lawson & Company. He also currently lectures on entrepreneurship for the Wharton School (as an adjunct faculty member). Rob is a founding member of Robin Hood Ventures (www.robinhoodventures.com), an angel investor group focused on emerging growth companies. Rob holds a BSE from the Wharton School and a BAS from the Engineering School of the University of Pennsylvania.

What was the most difficult part of raising capital?

The process from signing the term sheet to actually closing the deal. I am involved with a company called Knoa (*www.knoa.com*), and when we went to raise money, I had to write to 10 venture capitalists before one would speak with me. Once the fund had an interest, it took another three months to get a term sheet. The sailing was anything but smooth. It took about nine months from the time we started contacting venture capitalists until we actually raised the money.

What surprised you about the process?

That different investors took different approaches to when they would offer a term sheet. Some do it very early—before they have completed even basic due diligence—to see if it is worth spending their time on the deal. Others do a lot of due diligence first. But in all cases, the term sheet is only their start of negotiations and they will often change the terms along the way of the deal.

How important was having a business plan?

Critical. Can't even think about raising money without one. There are exceptions to this, of course. Steve Jobs or Jim Barksdale don't need much of a plan, but the rest of us do.

Did they actually read your plan?

It depends on the firm and the person in the firm. Usually, the junior person in the firm reads the entire plan, cover to cover. Some senior-level people do also. However, valuation was all over the map. Typically it's presented by the investor. As we had a track record, and prior financings, we were able to use the last financing as a benchmark in our valuation discussion.

How flexible did you have to be in negotiations?

Like Gumby.

What issues should an entrepreneur be aware of when reviewing a term sheet?

The amount of money and valuation are only a small part of the term sheet. Look for other governance items that effectively give the new investor control of the business. Make sure that these don't inhibit flexibility in attracting management and new investors.

Confirm that the investor is able to offer the deal presented and does not have an internal approval process that is not yet complete.

Confirm that the investor has the cash to invest.

Set deadlines for everything.

What is the most frustrating part of raising capital?

There are a lot of inexperienced people in the process—junior people at the VC and attorney level—who can really slow down and muck up a deal. This inexperience creates a lot of additional work and hassle.

If you had one piece of advice to give an entrepreneur raising capital, what would it be?

Don't box yourself out of having competition for any deal you are in. Don't let the investors exclude competition without short time frames on backing out of the deal.

SIXTY-FIVE QUESTIONS INVESTORS AND VENTURE CAPITALISTS ASK

You won't find them in a venture capitalists bureau or website, but there are basically 65 questions every investor wants answers to. Here is a list of the most common questions you will be asked by an investor regardless of what type of business you are in:

Problem

- What is the problem you are trying to solve?
- Who really needs it?

Business Description

- Briefly describe what your business does.
- Does the business have any past history?

Critical Success Factors

- What factors will determine if the business succeeds or fails?
- What keeps you up at night?
- How will you overcome barriers to success?

Competition

- How many direct competitors and indirect competitors are there?
- Who are they?
- What makes them special?
- How many customers do they have?
- What is their revenue?

Competitive Advantage

- What is your competitive advantage?
- Is it technology?
- Is anything you're developing patentable?
- Is it exclusive agreements?
- What is the barrier to entry you have erected?

Market

- What is the market for your service/product?
- How much does the average target company spend?
- Is it a growing or consolidating market?

Revenue

- How do you make money?
- What brings you the greatest source of revenue?
- Will technology make obsolete any source of revenue you are projecting?
- Will technology create new sources of revenue not listed here?

Marketing

- How will you market the company?
- Will you use print media?
- Will you run a direct mail campaign?

- Will you run a direct e-mail campaign?
- Will you use television and radio?
- How much will you need to spend in marketing to make your projections?

Sales

- How will the service be sold?
- How many salespeople will you need?
- Will your salespeople work out of an office or out of their homes?
- Will they be geographically dispersed?
- What types of backgrounds are you looking for?
- Does your head of sales have a lot of experience in this market space?
- How long will it typically take to sign a member?
- Will you develop an affiliates program?
- Will you develop strategic partnerships?
- What are your customer acquisition costs?

Retention

- What is the turnover rate in an industry such as yours?
- What tactics will you use to retain customers?
- Will you have someone in charge of retention?
- How much will you be spending on customer retention?

Management

- Who is filling the roles of president, vice president of marketing, vice president of sales, chief information officer, chief technology officer, chief financial officer, and vice president of client services?
- What type of business experience does each person have?
- Has the president ever grown a business to the size of the one you are projecting in your plan?

Board of Directors

- How many people are on your board?
- Who is on your board?
- What is their experience related to your business?

Technology

- How was your website developed?
- Who developed it?
- How many databases do you have and are they proprietary?
- What are the databases written in?
- How much experience do your CIO and CTO have at building these types of systems?

Launch Plan

- When will your site be ready for users to take advantage of it?
- When will you sign your first customer?

Financial Projections

- How much revenue will you bring in by year 5?
- When will you break even?
- When will you be cash flow positive?
- How much money do you realistically think it will take to obtain the revenues you project?

Investment

- How much money are you looking for?
- How do you plan to spend the money?
- How much equity are you willing to give up for what you are looking for?

Exit Strategy

- What is the exit strategy (go public or be bought out)?

VENTURE CAPITALIST ADVICE ON PRESENTATIONS

Dr. Brenda Gavin became president of S.R. One, Limited, in 1999. She had been a vice president with S.R. One since 1989. Prior to joining S.R. One, Brenda was director of business development for SmithKline Beecham Animal Health Products. She sits on the corporate boards of Message Pharmaceuticals, MircoMass Communications, Physician Verification Services, Oxis International, Synbiotics Corp., and Therion Biologics Corp. Dr. Gavin received a BS from Baylor University, a DVM from the University of Missouri, and an MBA from the University of Texas in San Antonio.

Should you bring overheads or do a PowerPoint presentation from your computer?

You should have some sort of presentation and you should have a hard copy to give to the venture capitalists. What you don't want to do is have a PowerPoint presentation that doesn't work. If you don't have a backup, then you really look dumb.

How long should your presentation be?

The presentation shouldn't be more than 45 minutes. Don't drag on and on. Save time for discussion about the business and the terms of the deal. Don't spend too much time on the product and/or technology.

I detest presentations that start with little building blocks if I don't know where they are going. I like to hear the overall concept or the endpoint first. Then go back and build up the story from the beginning. Tell us why the product is unique and why you are the team to do it. I like a little bit of history of the company and I like to know where the technology comes from. How did the company get started and what excited people about the technology or business?

How many people should you bring for a presentation?

Don't bring more than three people. Usually two will do. It should be the president/CEO and the person in charge of business development and/or marketing. For dot.com companies, we have to be convinced that the Internet really adds value and is not just another distribution channel. We also have to believe there is a real market there. Often, companies can convince us of Internet value and market size, but have no idea how to access that market. Many companies have no idea of their path to the market, or if they do have an idea, it is too expensive or impractical to implement.

How many people should speak?

You can have two people speak or one speak and both answer questions. If one person is more technically fluent or has a better understanding of the marketing, then both people should speak.

Should you provide handouts in the beginning or at the end?

You should definitely provide handouts in the beginning. This will allow the VC to make notes on the presentation.

Should you wear a suit to a presentation?

You can wear whatever you are comfortable in.

What mistakes do entrepreneurs typically make in a presentation?

The biggest mistake is that they don't answer the questions asked. They go in 10 different directions. Answer my question first, but if you don't know, then say you don't know. Just get to the point, and if you need to back up your answer with details, then do so.

The second biggest mistake is dot.com guys talk about how the Internet will make life easier, but they don't talk about how they are going to implement the plan. This says to me that they really don't believe in their plan as an ongoing business, but have just written something that gets them to IPO and exit.

CHAPTER SUMMARY

I can't emphasize enough the need for preparation. Every entrepreneur I have ever worked with or watched present who hadn't practiced and didn't anticipate the questions that would be asked never received investment. Remember the seven basic rules for presenting to potential investors:

1. *Practice presentations.* Don't make your first presentation to your most likely investors. Try to get in front of investors who would have a mild interest and let them critique your plan and presentation.

2. *Give handouts.* Provide question-and-answer handouts focused on the 65 questions I have provided in this chapter.

3. *Present a team effort.* Bring one or two members of your executive team and empower them to do part of the presentation and answer questions related to their expertise. If you bring two people, let each person take a section of the presentation.

4. *Don't deny competitors.* Don't tell investors that you don't have any competitors. You will lose all credibility. Everyone has some sort of competitors, whether they are direct or indirect.

5. *Understand your investor.* Find out before you meet what your investors like to invest in and, just as important, what turns them off.

6. *Know your financials.* Nothing kills a presentation more quickly than an entrepreneur who doesn't understand and can't explain her own financials.

7. *Focus.* Speak slowly, don't get frazzled, and think through each part of your presentation and each answer.

Follow the above rules and you will enhance your chances of obtaining funding. Don't follow them and you won't have any shot at getting funding.

10

NONVENTURE
FINANCING

There are five sources of financing that are nonventure-capital-related that most Internet entrepreneurs overlook when trying to find capital to launch their businesses. The sources are debt financing, public funding, vendor funding, receivable factoring, and joint ventures. Many manufacturers and suppliers are interested in using the Internet as one of their means of distribution. According to the Boston Consulting Group, less than 20% of manufacturers have websites, so this presents an opportunity to those entrepreneurs who are willing to build e-commerce sites.

These are good sources of funding to start with because they are quicker to obtain than venture capital financing, which could take up to a year. As anyone who has worked for an Internet company, bought Internet stocks, or even just used the Internet knows, one year is the equivalent of six in any other industry. Therefore, leverage every type of funding source to move your business concept ahead until you are able to bring in private, institutional, or corporate venture capital. Here are descriptions of each source of nonventure financing.

BANK FINANCING

Everyone is familiar with bank financing because everyone in business has bought a car or a house, or taken a loan to put themselves or their children through college. Bank financing is the least expensive form of financing.

THE PROCESS

Banks require collateral in the form of cash, property, or business contracts. Many people are not aware that you can borrow money against a business contract. If you have a government contract or a contract with a major corporation that guarantees payment, banks will provide funding to fulfill those contracts. The amount a company can borrow against a contract or property is usually 80% of the value of the contract or property.

PREPARATION EXPECTATIONS

Banks require forms to be filled out. These forms ask questions about the company's sales, future projections of sales, and available corporate and personal assets to be used as collateral for a loan. If the company or management is putting up property as collateral, banks need to see a title or deed. They will then send out an independent appraiser to evaluate the property. Most commercial lenders who finance troubled companies want to see a business plan. The bank won't make a loan if it doesn't think the company is capable of running the business properly and therefore able to pay back the loan. In addition, banks don't want to loan money to a company in a dying industry.

Large commercial banks also have workout departments. Workout departments specialize in working with distressed companies. They have bankers and consultants trained to handle troubled companies. These professionals mostly focus on how to cut expenses and reorganize existing loans.

ADVANTAGES

When interest rates are low, bank financing is very economical. Banks usually don't require equity in a company. Occasionally, banks will lend money and require warrants in the company. A *warrant* allows the bank to buy stock in the company at a specified or discounted price. If the company runs into trouble and can't make its payments, banks will sometimes restructure the loan or allow the company to pay only the interest.

DISADVANTAGES

If the company isn't able to repay its loans, the guarantors of the loan can lose their homes and equity in the business.

How to Keep Them Happy

Besides keeping monthly payments current, send the company's loan officer monthly financial statements and written reports on how the company is doing. Let the bank know what accounts you are targeting, because they may be able to make introductions or say something positive that will help open up new opportunities or close sales.

Internet Addresses

The address for the American Business Funding Directory is *abfd.netcom.com*. It provides the user with commercial bank contacts.

PUBLIC FUNDING

There are two types of government funding. The first is loans guaranteed by the Small Business Administration (SBA), and the second is loans and grants provided by states.

The Process

There are two types of funding programs: federal and state. The federal funding program is through the SBA. The SBA, working through commercial banks, guarantees loans that banks may not want to make on their own. The company must have collateral and must fill out various forms. Some states, such as Pennsylvania and Ohio, offer loan and grant programs. Funding requests over $25,000 usually require collateral or some amount of matching capital.

Preparation Expectations

Both state and federal programs want to see the same type of business plans that venture capitalists and investor angels require.

Advantages

Management doesn't have to give up equity.

Disadvantages

Management can lose its collateral with an SBA loan. Some state programs require capital, but by and large most don't.

How to Keep Them Happy

Keep in touch with the company loan officer or granting organization by telephone or invite him to the company offices. He will require some type of monthly or quarterly report, so make sure he receives it. Let him know if things aren't going well, so he can try to help and won't be shocked if the company can't pay back the loan.

Internet Address

sbaonline.sba.gov and *benfranklin.org*
On the Ben Franklin site is a link to a national network of private investors called the Angel Capital Electronic Network.

VENDOR FUNDING

Vendors will, on occasion, accept stock in lieu of payments if they believe the business is synergistic with their business or has a lot of upside potential to buy products/services in the future.

The Process

If the company cannot afford to make payments to its vendors and the vendor's products are crucial to the company's business, ask them if they will exchange debt for stock in the company. However, be prepared—most vendors will probably say no. GE Investments, the money management arm of General Electric, was started during the Depression because GE saw the advantage of taking stock in lieu of payment from businesses and industries they believed had growth potential. GE and other large companies are still open to funding customers who they believe have a lot of upside potential.

Preparation Expectations

Like everyone else, the vendor will want to see a business plan, but it will also want to know how much management expects to buy from it over a five-year period.

Advantages

It is a great way to reduce debt, and vendors can often provide prospect leads.

Disadvantages

There's another shareholder to answer to.

How to Keep Them Happy

Provide them with monthly reports and sales leads.

Internet Address

Not applicable.

FACTORING

Factors lend money using a company's accounts receivables as collateral.

The Process

A factor has the owner fill out forms that personally guarantee repayment of the loan. The factor has the owner sign a paper that allows it to run financial checks on the company's clients. If the clients are good payers, the factor will lend 70 to 80% of the value of the accounts receivable at a rate of 3% per month. This translates into an effective borrowing rate of 36% per year.

The owner must provide the factor with copies of all accounts receivable invoices, regardless of whether they are factored. The invoices must also contain the address of the factor, which will receive all future payments until the relationship is over. When the factor receives the balance of the receivable, it repays the company the remaining 17% of the invoice. If the payment is made after 30 days, the factor tacks on a 1% late penalty.

Preparation Expectations

Factors want to receive the business plan and past and current accounts receivables. They want a list of the current accounts receivable contacts along with their addresses.

Advantages

This is a great source for short-term capital. Once the relationship is set up, a company can receive money within 24 hours of every invoice sent out that was accepted by the factor. Outside of the clothing industry, most factors will tell their clients that if the client is using factoring for more than a year, there is something wrong with the business. They also may come across potential clients for their customers.

A client of mine wouldn't have survived without the ability to factor receivables. The firm she used was run by experienced business professionals, and they provided both money and business advice. Good factors provide more than money, because most factors have run or worked with a variety of businesses.

Disadvantages

The annual interest rate is 36% on a compounded basis.

How to Keep Them Happy

Make sure the address of the factor is on the invoice and let the factor know immediately if any mistakes in billing have been made or if the ability to collect will be a problem. Most factors are former bankers and businesspeople; therefore, use their knowledge and experience when tackling problems.

INTERNET ADDRESS

amer-rec.com

JOINT VENTURES

Joint ventures involve partnering between companies where all sides add value.

THE PROCESS

Management seeks out a company that could use its service or product to enhance business. My client, who ran a website development company, looked for companies that developed computer databases and that needed a partner company to develop the interface and content for the databases. She approached companies whose skills complemented, not competed with, her company's.

PREPARATION EXPECTATIONS

Joint venture partners want to know that their partners are knowledgeable and dependable. They want examples of work that the company has done previously, and contact names for previous customers. Give them a thorough written and verbal presentation describing what the company can do and how management sees the partner benefiting through this relationship.

One of the firms my website development client partnered with was a computer hardware company. This hardware company supplied my client with both hardware and software. My client developed a website that provided a critical outlet for the hardware company's products. Both parties realized that working together would enhance their chances for acquiring and retaining clients.

ADVANTAGES

You're able to leverage each partner's capabilities without having to buy or create that capability. Joint venture partners can open up doors to new opportunities and, in some cases, lead to a partner's offer to become a strategic investor. Microsoft is famous for doing this, as demonstrated by its buying stakes in such companies as Apple Computer and Comcast, one of the largest cable television operators in the world.

DISADVANTAGES

Management has to be wary of companies that are more excited about putting a partnership together than actually making them work. Management also has to be aware of potential partners whose real intention might be to learn someone else's business so they can move into that market. Therefore, management should never share its product development process or service methodology. This is difficult to do with international corporate partners.

It's easier to put together partnerships than to share information. The reason is that marketing people love to develop partnerships in the hope that those partnerships will produce business or keep a competitor away from a potentially good source of sales leads. Research and development people are concerned with guarding company secrets and worry that partners will take what they learn from the partnership and compete against the company.

HOW TO KEEP THEM HAPPY

Management needs to do only three things to keep partners happy:

- Do quality work.
- Stay ahead of the learning curve.
- Bring them new business.

INTERNET ADDRESS

Not applicable.

CHAPTER SUMMARY

Don't overlook nonventure-capital funding sources. If you do, you may lose your opportunity. Not all nonventure-capital funding sources require you to take on debt. Look at the following sources and see how they fit into your overall financing strategy:

- Debt financing
- Public funding
- Vendor funding
- Receivable factoring
- Joint ventures

Some of these sources of funding could open doors with equity investors that they have contact with, or they themselves might convert their debt to equity if the e-commerce site looks as if it has a lot of upside potential.

11

PRIVATE INVESTOR CAPITAL

When most people think of financing a startup venture, they immediately think of institutional venture capital. The truth is that private investors fund more Internet startups than professional and corporate venture capitalists. Most venture capitalists would rather see an entrepreneur launch his company with capital from private investors than from venture capitalists. Once the website is up and running and demonstrating some level of need, then venture capitalists are willing to look and consider investing.

In 1990, I started and ran the Pennsylvania Private Investors Group (PPIG), which is now thriving, I have also helped to launch the Baltimore Private Investors Group. In my 15 years of dealing with private investors, I found that the typical profile for an investor is as follows:

- Usually is aged 40 to 60.

- Has large corporate or highly successful entrepreneurial experience.

- Usually has a net worth of $10 million or greater. When you have more than $10 million, you feel as if you can put $1 to $2 million in $50,000 to $100,000 increments to work in 20 to 40 companies. The law of averages is in your favor that you will get all of your original principal back and probably make a tidy profit and have fun doing it.

- Has worked in high-margin businesses. Individuals who worked in low-margin businesses have a greater fear that if they lose money it will be hard to make it back. They are also more averse to risk.

When I started PPIG, there were only a handful of private investor groups. Now practically every major city has a private investor group. Many banks and investment banks either bring deals to their clients on an informal basis or partner with other organizations such as accounting and law firms to pool resources and clients to fund new companies.

The investor angels that an e-commerce entrepreneur wants to attract are ones who have invested in Internet stocks, use the Internet to manage their investments, have bought products on the Internet, and have invested in at least one Internet startup. The investor should also bring management and industry expertise. If you are developing an e-commerce site to sell antiques, find an investor who has bought and sold antiques and has experienced the Internet.

INVESTOR ANGEL GROUPS

According to Jeffrey E. Sohl, director of the Center for Venture Research at the Whittemore School of Business and Economics at the University of New Hampshire, there are over 400,000 active private investors a year out of a total of 2 million total individuals who qualify as accredited investors ($2 million net worth or $250,000-plus income after taxes). Private investors, according to Professor Sohl, invest $30–40 billion per year in 50,000 ventures.

THE PROCESS

You provide your potential investors with a business plan and review it with them. Normally, you state in your plan how much capital you plan to raise and the minimum amount you need to raise before you can touch any new money that has been invested. Private placements can range from $50,000 to millions of dollars.

Investors receive common or preferred stock, or a combination of both, and in some cases warrants for additional shares as well. Preferred stock usually involves some rate of guaranteed interest paid on the invested funds. Warrants allow earlier buyers of the stock a chance to buy additional shares at the same price should the value of the shares rise.

Before raising private capital, speak to a securities attorney to make sure you are following the laws of the state in which you are located. In addition, there are federal regulations that need to be followed.

Raising private capital can take as little as 30 days or as long as a year. Usually, if companies can raise capital within six months, they either don't need it or they are out of business.

PREPARATION EXPECTATIONS

Write a full business plan that shows past financial statements, current cash flow, and projected profit and loss for up to five years. Invite investors to the company's offices to meet your management team and the employees.

ADVANTAGES

Companies don't have to put up any collateral and can sometimes leverage the money raised in a private offering to get state grants.

DISADVANTAGES

Management can lose a lot of sleep taking other people's money, since most managers feel a personal sense of obligation. Sometimes private investors want a certain amount of control before they invest. They feel the need to protect themselves in case you make bad decisions. This control can come in the form of having board seats and voting control of the company. Conceivably, the owner can be removed without cause.

Make sure you know about the investor's business savvy, experience, and mental makeup before you take her money. An investor could become a major thorn in management's side if she can't afford to lose the money or doesn't understand the business.

HOW TO KEEP THEM HAPPY

Make them feel that they are part of the company's extended family. For instance, send them the same reports the company would send to its banker. Find out what contact investors may have that can lead to additional sales. Investors will put in more capital if they see that management is making the right decisions, even if the decisions aren't panning out immediately.

INTERNET ADDRESS

There are three ways to find investor angels:

1. The Small Business Administration *(www.sbaonline.com)* provides links to investor angel networks in Massachusetts, New Hampshire, Pennsylvania, and Texas.

2. Online services that link entrepreneurs to private investors include *www.vcapital.com*, *www.capmatch.com*, *www.offroadcapital.com*, *www.capital.com*, *www.garage.com*, and *www.datamerge.com*.

3. There are local investor angel groups scattered throughout the country: Robin Hood Ventures *(www.robinhoodventures.com)*, Pennsylvania Private Investors Group *(www.ppig.com)*, Alliance of Angels *(www.allianceangels.com)*, Atlanta Technology Angels *(www.angelatlanta.com)*, Tech Coast Angels *(www.techcoastangels. org)*, The Capital Network *(www.texasangelinvestors.org)*, Silicon Alley Venture Partners *(www.savp.com)*, and Angel Investor Funding *(www.angelinvestorfunding.com)*.

When approaching various private investor groups and online services, keep in mind that private investors typically don't like to invest in companies that are more than a two-hour drive from their homes. Private investors like to be able to see and touch the companies they invest in. If you are unaware of any private investor groups in your region, contact your local chamber of commerce or the region's largest law and accounting firms. They should know if one exists in your area.

PRIVATE INVESTOR'S EXPECTATIONS

Vincent G. Bell, Jr., began his business career as co-founder of a general construction company in 1954. Vincent co-founded Safeguard Business Systems, Inc., in 1956, and over 30 years grew it to $300 million in revenue, providing manual and computerized products and services to more than 1 million small businesses and professionals in the United States, Canada, and the United Kingdom. Vincent was chairman and CEO of Safeguard Business Systems until its sale to a Texas merchant bank in 1986. He has personally *invested his own money in 25 companies, currently serves on the boards of Envirite Corporation, Safeguard Scientifics, Inc., and Elity Systems, Inc., and is an advisor to Safeguard Business Systems, Inc. Vincent is a graduate of Lehigh University with a degree in mechanical engineering.*

How important is a business plan?

We won't invest without a business plan. The angels group I am involved with called LORE won't look at the entrepreneurs until they have developed a plan. They are important because they are a discipline that forces entrepreneurs to see what is in front of them. The plans are seldom met, but it helps them figure out who their competitors are and determine their marketing plans and what cash they need to grow the business. You don't live or die by the plan since I have never seen a business go completely according to plan.

Does a plan with beautiful graphics and color influence your decision to invest?

It would frighten me. It is a negative. They aren't spending their time on the right things. I would worry about where their priorities are.

Have you ever invested in a company that didn't provide a business plan?

I have been in some situations that were such raw startups that they didn't start with a plan, but within a couple of months we had a plan. I have never been involved with a company that didn't have a plan within the first quarter of its existence.

What types of skills do you look for in the entrepreneurs you invest in?

I look for persistence. They all have ideas, but most companies have gone through the "valley of the shadow of death"—something has gone wrong and only the best keep their operations alive. It isn't a skill. It is a characteristic.

How important is it for the leader to be charismatic?

It is extremely helpful. It can make up for a lot of other deficiencies. Is it the most essential ingredient? No! The role of the entrepreneur is to be a leader. It's easier if you have a lot of charisma, but at the end of the day smart people follow good ideas and sound thinking.

How important is it to have prior management experience?

It is very important. You can't build a successful business without hiring great people and having the skills to manage them. You can do it without management experience, but it makes it a lot easier.

How important is it to have experience in the field you are looking to launch a company in?

That is critical. It's one thing you can't fake. You'd better know what is going on or you can be easily misled. You don't need to know generic skills like financing and marketing, but you need to know about how your industry works.

What are the characteristics of the entrepreneurs you have invested in who have succeeded?

They come up with a good idea that is appropriate for the marketplace. They somehow get enough resources to see if the idea works or not. They are persistent and determined regardless of the difficulty. They are willing to accept change. They have to be flexible in the approaches they take. They have sensitivity to their environment and can detect changes that most people miss.

What were the shortcomings of the entrepreneurs you invested in who didn't make it?

Most fail because they don't understand finance. They don't know how to run a business. Worse, they believe that they do know it or they don't think it is important and then they run into real trouble.

Before making an investment, do you insist on meeting the rest of the management team?

I generally try to do it, but sometimes I haven't. I would suggest to others investing that they insist upon it.

How important is it that board members have invested their own cash?

It sure brings reality to the situation and I think it is critical. You can look beyond the cash if they have significant contacts, but they should invest something regardless of how minimal that investment is.

What is a realistic amount of money that an entrepreneur should expect to raise from private investors?

Entrepreneurs should look to raise $300,000 to $500,000 in the seed stage. Maybe you can raise as much as $1 million, but that is tough.

What should an entrepreneur look for in an investor besides capital?

It would be great if the investor knew something about the industry or had a particular experience that added value.

What types of investors should an entrepreneur be wary of?

A pure financial investor who is trying to turn a quick dollar. I would worry about guys with little business experience. You have to worry about people who are highly intelligent and think they know everything.

SMALL COMPANIES OFFERING REGISTRATION (SCOR)

SCOR is a public state registration through which companies can raise up to $1 million per year. It is a financial vehicle set up for small companies to raise money through individual private investors. The investors do not have to be accredited, which means they don't have to have a minimum net worth of $2 million or $250,000 in disposable income. Most states now have provisions for SCOR offerings. The requirements for the legal and accounting work are minimal and the approval process is streamlined.

The Process

Filling out a SCOR is similar to developing a prospectus to go public. Every state has certain requirements, so the best way to make sure the company is in compliance is to contact a securities attorney in the state where the company is headquartered. Also speak with the state's securities office, which can be found by contacting the state's department of commerce. SCOR is controlled by each individual state.

Advantages

It is not as cumbersome or as expensive as doing a public offering.

DISADVANTAGES

There is no downside.

To use SCOR to raise capital, contact a securities attorney and have him give you the proper forms for an offering.

CHAPTER SUMMARY

Raising money from private investors gives an entrepreneur instant credibility. Ways to raise money from private investors include the following:

- Approach regional private investor groups.

- Apply through an online venture matching service.

- Contact service providers who work with wealthy, experienced business executives.

- Put together a Small Companies Offering Registration, which will increase the pool of potential investors by allowing the entrepreneur to take money from nonaccredited investors.

Before taking money from private investors, make sure that you speak to your attorney and that you have developed a private placement memorandum that meets state and federal securities regulations. Finally, the value of taking money from private investors, according to Vincent "Buck" Bell, Jr., is that it gives a venture "the mark of quality that someone has the courage to put in money."

12

INSTITUTIONAL
CAPITAL

Every entrepreneur who writes a business plan and launches an e-commerce company wants and, in most cases, needs to raise institutional capital. The reason most companies need institutional capital is that they need $5 million to $100 million to build the business before the company has a public offering or is sold to a strategic partner. Four types of institutional capital will be covered in this chapter:

- Traditional venture capital
- Corporate venture capital
- Publicly traded shells
- Small companies offering registration

As was mentioned earlier in the book, less than six-tenths of 1% of business plans are funded by institutional venture capital.

TRADITIONAL VENTURE CAPITAL

Traditional venture capitalists invest money provided by pension funds and wealthy individuals. They have a specific investment focus in terms of the life cycle of the business (seed, early, and later stage) and industry focus (software, Internet, telecommunications, etc.).

THE PROCESS

Venture capitalists review the company business plan and then decide if they want to visit the company and interview the management team. If they believe management's plan and see the potential to go public or sell the company at some point, then they may invest. It can take from 90 days, if they love the company, to six months to get venture capital.

Once venture capitalists decide to invest, they will provide a legal document to sign. This document typically provides them with controls to protect their investment. An example may be the ability to remove the president for poor performance. Venture capitalists want warrants to buy additional shares at the current price and a nondilution clause if the owner needs to raise additional capital.

PREPARATION EXPECTATIONS

Management needs to provide venture capitalists with a business plan showing a one-year cash flow and five-year financial projections. Nobody will believe your numbers, but they want to understand how you arrived at those numbers and if the opportunity is large enough to warrant an investment.

A few years ago, venture capitalists were investing in e-commerce companies that didn't show a profit within five years. Today a company has to project that it will break even within three years and be profitable within its fourth or fifth year. Before meeting with the venture capitalists, ask them for references and make sure you will be comfortable with them.

ADVANTAGES

Management doesn't have to provide collateral, although most venture capitalists will expect that management have its personal cash invested. Venture capitalists have a lot of business experience and contacts.

DISADVANTAGES

If management isn't meeting the sales plan of the company or doesn't appear to be the right group to take the company to the next level, then management risks being removed as head of the company. The president may also be forced to sell the company before he is ready.

How to Keep Them Happy

Have lunch with venture capitalists once a month and provide them with a written report and financial statements. Don't treat them as if the only value they have is the money they're able to invest. Leverage their contacts and experience.

Internet Address

National Venture Capital Association *(www.nvca.org).*

THE VENTURE CAPITALIST'S DUE DILIGENCE PROCESS

One of the great secrets or unknowns to entrepreneurs looking for capital is the process venture capitalists take once they have received a business plan. I contacted Peter Ligeti, a partner in one of Philadelphia's oldest venture capital funds, Keystone Venture Capital. The Keystone's due diligence process has 30 steps in total.

The 10 major events are as follows:

1. Log in business plan.
2. Review plan and fill out review sheet.
3. If the plan meets the muster of the first partner, then a second partner reads the plan.
4. Once the plan is reviewed by two partners and there is sufficient interest, then a partner has a telephone conversation with the entrepreneur to ask some additional qualifying questions.
5. After speaking with the entrepreneur, the venture capitalist speaks to industry experts.
6. If the industry experts speak highly of the concept, then the venture capitalist meets with the entrepreneur.
7. If the venture capitalist likes what she hears and finds out, then a term sheet is offered.
8. The venture capitalist and entrepreneur negotiate the terms.
9. A term sheet is executed.
10. A deal is closed.

Keystone Venture Capital's Due Diligence Flow Chart

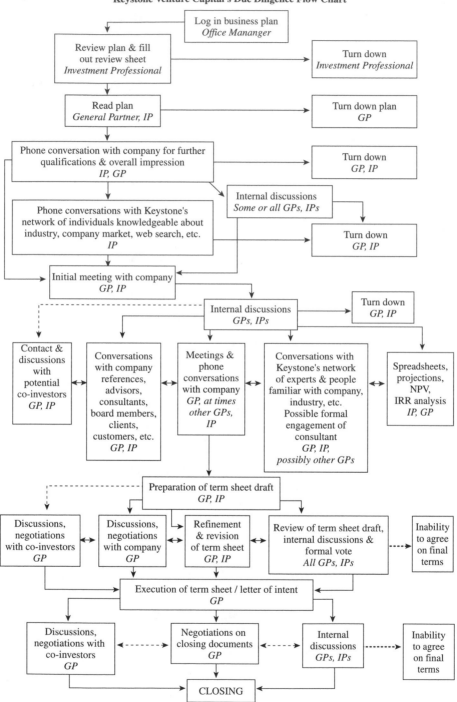

Many of my clients don't realize that just getting a venture capitalist to review their deal is difficult, but even more difficult is getting through all the steps that will eventually lead to a meeting. The chances of getting an actual term sheet are about the same as making the roster of a National Football League team. According to Ken Anderson, managing editor of Venture Wire, slightly less than 5,000 deals will be consummated in 2000 and less than 20% are B2B or B2C deals.

On the opposite page is a chart of the Keystone Venture Capital's due diligence process.

VENTURE CAPITAL BUSINESS PLAN QUESTIONS

Glenn Rieger, who was interviewed in Chapter 2, has read thousands of business plans over the past 10 years as both an investment banker and a venture capitalist. He knows as well as anyone in the country what will encourage a venture capitalist to support a new venture.

What is more important: the concept or the management team?

There is no idea so good that a management team can't destroy it. Good management can take a mediocre product and make it a success. Just look at Microsoft. No one says it's a great product, but it dominates the world.

How important is it to have selected and gotten commitments from the entire management team?

I don't have enough bandwidth to help an entrepreneur put a team together. If someone comes without a management team, it is hard to put him at the top of the pile when a dozen other good plans have complete teams. The entrepreneur can identify people who work for other people, but I need to be able to call for references and other information.

What type of financial information do you require? Five years out and one-year cash flow?

We don't *require* a one-year cash flow or five-year financial projection. Typically, plans come with this detail. The most important thing is to get the first meeting. We won't decide whether or not to take a meeting based on financials. We will take the meeting based on opportunity, management, and market. I have seen where entrepreneurs have underestimated the market. I have seen plans where I perceived a strategic fit with another company and the company hadn't considered that relationship.

Should an entrepreneur hire an accountant to develop its financials?

No! The kiss of death is when the entrepreneur says that he can't explain the financials and that the accountant put together the financials. Entrepreneurs need to be intimately involved and able to explain their own financials.

Should an entrepreneur hire a national accounting firm to audit its books or will a local firm be acceptable?

A local accounting firm is fine in the beginning. Entrepreneurs don't need a Big Five firm until they get major revenue and have stock option issues. They should use small firms and save themselves money.

Should entrepreneurs hire an attorney with venture capital experience?

They should absolutely hire an attorney familiar with venture capital. We don't want to have to educate the entrepreneur's attorney. The attorney who doesn't know the venture game can kill a deal.

How important is it to have selected board members?

I think it is important. You need to leave some spots open for your investors because they will require them.

What type of board members should one try to attract?

You should look for people who have relevant experience with their marketplace. Don't pad your board with friends and family. You need people who can open doors and create relationships. I don't sweat the fact that the board member hasn't put money in the business. I do question how much time and energy they are going to give to the company.

Should you ask for more money than you need?

You should definitely ask for more than you need; you never know when the funding window is going to dry up. You need to support what you are asking for. You need to know what you really want.

What are the chances that a VC will review a plan that isn't sent to the fund by someone the fund knows?

We review every plan. We receive about 20 plans a week. Venture funds that get an enormous number of plans have a hard time reviewing all of the plans. That is why it is important to get your message across concisely in the first few pages.

How important is it to have someone who knows venture capitalists endorse your plan?

If someone I trust asks me to review a plan, I will give it a careful and extraconsiderate read.

In a high-tech venture, what percentage of the overall budget should be spent on marketing?

That will differ company by company. There is no rule of thumb.

How detailed should the launch plan be?

Since we invest in most second rounds, we come in after the launch. I want to see the results of the launch. There needs to be enough detail to know they can accomplish their task at hand.

How soon would you like to realize the return on your investment?

It is not unrealistic for a VC to want to see a return in two to three years. As an entrepreneur, you need to know how old the fund is that you are approaching. At the extreme, you don't want to bring a biotech fund that will take 10 years to exit or a fund that is in the sixth year of its 10-year limited life. In most cases, you are looking at an 18-month–to–three-year exit scenario.

What is the return you aim for when making these investments (e.g., five times amount invested)?

We look for 10 times our money.

What are the major factors you use to determine a company's valuation?

It differs company by company. We look at public company comparables. We look at comparable transactions. We look at an industry-specific matrix. In the Internet world it used to be things such as page views. It depends on the business and industry. It's a waste of time to use a valuation company because it probably has been paid for by the entrepreneur.

What are the characteristics of the entrepreneurs you have invested in that have succeeded?

They will brave through any storm. They are very entrepreneurial. They will work any number of hours it takes to succeed. They have a clear vision and they are agile and can move with the changes. They do whatever it takes to succeed.

What were the shortcomings of the entrepreneurs you invested in who didn't make it?

Vision taken to an extreme is dangerous. This happens when you believe so much in what you are doing that you start to ignore advice from your investors and ignore feedback from the market. That is what usually kills most ventures.

Before making an investment, do you insist on meeting the rest of the management team?

Yes!

How important is it that board members have invested their own cash?

It's a consideration, but not critical.

What value do venture capitalists put on companies that raise private capital before going after institutional capital?

If the valuations the private investors bought in at are reasonable and the private investors are credible, that's a positive.

CORPORATE VENTURE CAPITAL

Since the mid-1990s, profits have been very good for most major corporations, and many of them have started venture capital funds such as J.P. Morgan (*www.labmorgan.com*), Cambridge Technology Partners (*www.ctp.com*),

Glaxo-SmithKline *(www.srone.com)*, and General Electric *(www.gecapital. com)*. Corporate venture funds look for strategic investments that can leverage their knowledge, industry contacts, and capabilities.

THE PROCESS

Their process is basically the same as that of traditional venture capitalists. They typically respond more quickly than traditional venture funds because many entrepreneurs don't know they exist. All of the deal documents are similar to traditional venture capitalists'.

PREPARATION EXPECTATIONS

Corporate venture capitalists want the same information as traditional venture capitalists. The difference when applying for corporate venture capital is that you need to demonstrate how the corporation can benefit through its investment in your company and what value the corporation can bring aside from its capital. When I approached J.P. Morgan's early-stage venture capital fund called LabMorgan, the first question they asked after we presented our concept was how could J.P. Morgan leverage its expertise and contacts to assist our business.

ADVANTAGES

The advantages of working with a corporate venture fund is that the company will only invest in businesses they understand and therefore will add a lot of value in terms of intellectual capital and contacts. The names of most corporations are better known than the names of traditional venture capital funds, so having a corporate venture partner adds a lot of cachet to the company. It can provide access to talented board members and potential employees.

DISADVANTAGES

The downside of a corporate investor is that if the parent company has financial troubles or new management takes over, the fund may not be able to invest. One of my clients was funded by a New York Stock Exchange company whose stock took a great tumble with all of the other technology stocks. The parent itself was in the process of raising money, and when the market tumbled, its potential investors left and that precluded them from investing more money in the companies they originally invested in. Now my client is scrambling to stay alive. Another potential disadvantage is the people assigned to work with your company may be overloaded with work and unable to provide you with the resources and time that you need.

How to Keep Them Happy

Don't tell the corporate venture fund you will use the company's resources just to get them to write the check. Take advantage of their expertise and see if you can outsource nonmission-critical functions such as accounting and human resources to the parent company while you focus on developing and marketing your site.

Internet Address

National Venture Capital Association *(www.nvca.org)*.

VENTURE LEASING

Venture leasing companies will provide the capital to lease equipment and software in exchange for equity or stock options and warrants for future equity. This type of leasing is for companies that can't obtain normal leases because of their credit situations.

The Process

Venture leasing companies work the same as regular leasing companies, except they are willing to take greater risks and usually don't require an individual to personally sign for a lease. Venture leasing companies are interested in reviewing the same business plans and financial statements as banks, venture capitalists, and investment bankers.

Preparation Expectations

The same information the company provided to an equity venture capitalist needs to be supplied to a venture leasing company.

ADVANTAGES

Venture leasing provides another source of capital to keep the business moving forward. Venture leasing companies also see other opportunities and may be able to make introductions that can lead to new business.

DISADVANTAGES

It is very expensive money. You will be paying a high interest rate because of the increased risk, and you will be giving up valuable equity that management might have been able to use to bring in another investor down the road.

HOW TO KEEP THEM HAPPY

Keep them informed as you would other investors by providing monthly financial statements and reports on the company's overall progress.

INTERNET ADDRESS

cfol.com/lists.htm

This includes a link to a website that has a database listing venture leasing companies throughout the United States.

Finally, remember that giving away equity can be more expensive than borrowing money in the long run, so be careful about whom management allows to invest and how much stock the company sells.

CHAPTER SUMMARY

Few, if any, companies that have gone public over the past 10 years have had to obtain institutional venture capital. By taking venture capital, an entrepreneur reaps the following benefits:

- New cash with no personal debt
- Validation that the business model has value
- Potential business contacts
- Access to experienced professionals

Remember there is a downside to taking institutional venture capital:

- You, and any partners you may have, don't own 100% of the company anymore.
- You have new partners that you have to report to.
- Institutional and corporate venture capitalists want to take the company public or sell their interest within three to five years, so you are under pressure to ramp up revenues quickly, which means long hours for you and your staff.

The best and brightest are attracted to venture-backed companies, so if you want to create personal wealth, this is the route to go.

13

CLOSING
THE DEAL

After the investors have reviewed the business plan and have listened to the entrepreneur's presentation, they typically will tell the entrepreneur that they are interested in investing. When an entrepreneur hears that an investor wants to invest, she is ready to pop the champagne and start hiring people. Any entrepreneur who has successfully gone through the process of raising capital will tell you that a deal is not complete until the money is in the company's bank account. The next leg in the journey to obtaining capital is to receive and agree on a term sheet provided by the investors.

WHAT IS A TERM SHEET?

The term sheet, according to John Delaney (one of the country's leading venture attorneys and a partner at Morrison & Forester), is sometimes referred to as a letter of intent, a memorandum of understanding, an agreement in principle, or, according to one judge, a "hug before marriage." A term sheet typically outlines the key points of a deal and identifies issues requiring further discussion. In the financing context, a term sheet outlines the major points of a contemplated financing transaction, and serves as a basis from which the ultimate transaction documents are drafted.

Term sheets are also intended to allow either party to walk away unscathed from the bargaining table if the negotiations break down (i.e., they are nonbinding). However, a term sheet sometimes contains specific binding provisions that will give rise to breach of contract claims if violated (e.g., breakup fees, no-shop periods, and confidentiality provisions).

An important fact to keep in mind, according to Delaney, is that no matter how much a venture capitalist tells you that he is interested in your company, don't believe him until you receive a draft term sheet! Venture capitalists have a vested interest in never saying no to a company— although they may not be interested in you at this time, next week the market may shift and suddenly your business model will become appealing to the venture capitalist. Moreover, venture capitalists can have a "herd mentality"—that is, they are not truly interested in your company unless someone else becomes interested. If your company suddenly becomes hot with other funds, the venture capitalist will want to be able to renew discussions with you (which will be much harder to do if the venture capitalist has already rejected you). As a result, venture capitalists like to string companies along, keeping them in limbo until the stars are properly aligned!

Experienced venture lawyers have all heard the enthusiastic young entrepreneur exclaim that such-and-such venture fund is "very interested in my company," yet, despite weeks of meetings and telephone calls, no term sheet has emerged—even though a draft term sheet takes only a few hours to prepare! In such situations, the lawyer will usually encourage the entrepreneur to focus on meeting with other venture funds.

After investors and the entrepreneur agree on terms, a provision will be in the term sheet that states the offer to invest will be contingent on the venture capitalist's performing due diligence. Due diligence is when the venture capitalist speaks to your potential customers, employees, past employers, and past partners; reviews the company's financial projections in depth; and makes an in-depth study of the competitors.

Many Internet deals collapse during due diligence for a variety of reasons. For example, the investors may find the entrepreneur not easy to work with, the management team may know less than the investors initially thought they knew about the business, or a group of better-financed competitors may have entered the field. Some of the reasons are within the control of the entrepreneur; others are not. When third parties are brought in by the investors to evaluate your business, you need to understand the personal and professional relationships the third party has with the investors so you don't blow the deal.

WHO CREATES THE TERM SHEET: THE VENTURE CAPITALIST OR THE ENTREPRENEUR?

Typically, the venture capitalist creates the term sheet, according to Delaney, because a term sheet is essentially an offer from a venture capitalist relating to the specifics of a proposed financing. In fact, sophisticated venture capitalists often prefer to create the term sheet because they have language and forms with which they are comfortable from prior use and prior legal review. In that sense, waiting for the venture capitalist to generate the term sheet may ultimately save the entrepreneur time as well as potential embarrassment from proposing terms that are far from what the venture capitalist had in mind. However, an entrepreneur might consider creating the term sheet when she is involved in an angel round, where the investors may not be as seasoned or don't have to abide by the same formalities as venture capitalists. Whether dealing with venture capitalists or angel investors, an entrepreneur will understandably feel compelled to create the term sheet in order to move the deal along, but should not do so without consulting an attorney, who may also have a collection of term sheets from previous deals.

FROM ACCEPTING A TERM SHEET TO SIGNING A DEAL, HOW LONG DOES THE PROCESS USUALLY TAKE?

There is no maximum—some deals take years to close, according to Delaney. Assuming that you have legal counsel dedicated to your transaction and the full attention of the venture capitalist and his legal counsel, the minimum you should expect is two weeks from signing the term sheet to closing the transaction. The typical time frame, however, is four to six weeks from the signing of the term sheet.

Common factors that can prolong the length of time between signing the term sheet and closing the deal include the following:

- Key "deal points" have not been agreed to up-front.
- The term sheet contains ambiguities or missing terms that need resolution.
- The venture capitalist's due diligence takes longer than expected or raises issues requiring further investigation or resolution (e.g., executive employees not having signed confidentiality or employment agreements, potentially infringing use of core intellectual property, financial statements lacking proper review by auditors).
- A party does not have negotiating leverage.
- A party has to obtain approval for new terms from its respective management or board.
- There is general market volatility.
- Venture capitalists may perceive a tactical advantage to dragging out negotiations, particularly if the startup company is running low on cash. By slowing down the process, the venture capitalist can demand more favorable terms as the company becomes more desperate to close the deal. Of course, reputable venture capitalists tend to see this as a shortsighted, misguided strategy—they want to put their money into strong companies, not weak ones.

WHAT COULD CAUSE MY DEAL TO FALL APART?

Ten obstacles or potential deal breakers that an entrepreneur has to clear before a deal can be consummated are as follows:

1. *Valuation.* The first question investors will ask is how much money are you looking for and how much of the company are you selling and at what price. One venture capitalist told me that his fund offered

a term sheet to an entrepreneur that was at a lower per share price than the entrepreneur was asking for. The venture capitalist assumed that the entrepreneur would come back with a counteroffer. Instead, the entrepreneur, believing the venture capitalist liked her deal so much that it would pay what she was asking, said the price per share was nonnegotiable. The venture capitalist said he was shocked by the response and walked away. The venture capitalist said other funds that were interested received the same response. Six months later the entrepreneur came back and said she was willing to negotiate; unfortunately, the market for her type of e-commerce company had changed and there were too many competitors.

2. *Management.* Many entrepreneurs hire top-level executives whom they don't know but were referred to them by someone they know and trust. The entrepreneur meets, interviews, and likes the executive, but hasn't taken or had the time to perform a serious background check. Before venture capitalists begin their due diligence, make sure you know the strengths and weaknesses of your own team. Be prepared to justify and defend why you picked specific people. Make sure you have thoroughly vetted their backgrounds.

You don't want venture capitalists to hit you with any surprises such as that one of your managers never did what he claimed to do on his resume. If the investors suggest that certain managers you have picked should be replaced for acceptable reasons, you need to listen and act. Loyalty to your employees is important, but getting funded is more important. I tell every potential employee that funding the business comes before anything else, and if the investors can reasonably justify why the potential employee isn't a good fit or say they can bring in someone better, then it is my responsibility to do what is best for the company and its investors.

3. *Competitors known and unknown.* Numerous times I have seen venture capitalists kill a deal because they viewed a company as a competitor to the company they were interested in investing in and management never considered the supposed competitor a threat. The best way to combat this is to ask the venture capitalist why he believes a particular

company is a threat and to give you time to assess the threat and respond. Both my clients and I have made the mistake of responding on the spot. Your answer may be the same a week later, but it will show the venture capitalists that you take the time to think before you react. Most times you will be able to logically explain why the perceived threat isn't a threat and in some cases is a potential ally.

Also, you had better know your competitors as well as they know themselves. You should take a look at your competitors' websites a minimum of once a week. The last thing you want to happen is that your investors ask you a question about a competitor that you could have answered if you had reviewed its website.

4. *Future investment.* It is extremely important to have investors that have the capability to invest additional money in a second round of financing. It looks bad to future investors if your first-round investors aren't willing to put in money to move the company to the next level. If your first-round investors are individuals, professional venture capitalists usually understand that individuals have limits in terms of what they can invest.

5. *Closing costs.* First-time entrepreneurs are usually surprised to find that they have to pay the venture capitalist's legal fees along with their own. I had a client whose attorney told the venture fund that if his client had to pay its attorney fees, the deal could fall apart. Fortunately, the venture capitalist contacted my client, explained the situation, and gave him the names of three other attorneys to speak with who would confirm what the venture capitalist had told him. Make sure you hire an experienced attorney who knows what the legitimate closing costs are.

6. *Board seats.* The investors, depending on the size of their investment and the percentage of the company they will own, will ask for the number of board seats that correspond to the size of their investment. For example, if there are six board seats and the investors will own half of the company's stock, then they will expect three board seats. Although investors have the final decision over who represents them, you want the

opportunity to meet their proposed board members and have input on their selection.

You don't want individuals whom you don't believe you can work with because of personality or professional differences. Insist on meeting all board members and give the investors the opportunity to interview your board members and suggest changes. You want a board that will work together for the good of the organization. One of my clients didn't ask to review the board members the investors proposed and assumed the board members the investor brought with it had the same view of the company as the investor did. Within the first two months, one of the new board members became so adversarial that my client was spending more time thinking about how to get rid of the board member than about how to grow the business.

7. *Rollout strategy.* Every e-commerce company has a rollout strategy regardless of whether its customers are regional or national. Make sure you understand your investor's hot buttons on this issue. One of the ventures I am involved in was negotiating with a venture fund whose money came from local-government pension funds. It was extremely important for the company to have its order fulfillment center nearby so that top pension fund officials could stop in and see the operation. The investor said his investors would have a higher degree of comfort if he could show them that jobs were being created in their area. If we had insisted that the fulfillment center be located in another area, they wouldn't have invested.

8. *Investment synergy.* For many investors, such as corporations and individuals, it is important that a prospective investment provide the opportunity to leverage the investor's assets and contacts and possibly add value to its existing investments. When you are going through the due diligence process, try to get an in-depth knowledge of the investors' backgrounds, what their strengths and weaknesses are, how your company could add value to their other investments, and which companies in the investors' portfolios failed and why. One of my clients received a term sheet with a large commercial bank and, during the due

diligence process, found out that the investor had had a bad experience with husband-and-wife teams.

My client went to the investor and acknowledged that she understood the investor had a bad experience with such teams, but my client highly valued her husband's involvement. She suggested to the investor that the husband could report to someone other than her and that the investors could review her husband's performance. If that wasn't acceptable, the husband said he would be willing to leave the company.

9. *Dilution.* Every professional investor has written into the term sheets that if the company's value doesn't increase when the entrepreneur needs the next round of funding, the entrepreneur, not the investor, is diluted. This means the entrepreneur has to sell his own stock. If the stock price goes up and the original investors want to hold on to the same percentage of stock, they have the option to buy additional stock at a discounted price. This is nonnegotiable.

10. *Financials.* Entrepreneurs should be prepared to defend every number in their projections. There is nothing wrong with updating financials during the due diligence process if it enhances the company's prospects for success. If you change the financials and the results indicate less revenue and/or greater losses, this could kill the investor's interest in investing. No entrepreneur or investor truly knows the positive or negative changes that new technology will have on the company. The best thing to do is only adjust the number if the results will be positive. Don't risk losing the investor on negative speculation.

EVALUATING YOUR COMPANY

Every entrepreneur I have ever worked with has asked me the same question before meeting with potential investors: How much should I value my company for? Most entrepreneurs take an unscientific approach. They put together their financials and then figure out how much money they need and put a value on it. Some entrepreneurs ask others who have received funding. What usually happens is the entrepreneur either undervalues or overvalues his company. I would strongly suggest, if you have the capital, that you hire an evaluation firm to develop a case for why your company is worth the stock price you are asking the venture capitalist to buy in at. Here is an interview with Doug Rogers of CBIZ Valuation Counselors, which has developed valuations for such companies as Lycos, CMGI, Agency.com, and Flycast Network.

Doug Rogers is executive vice president of CBIZ Valuation Counselors, one of the largest U.S. full-service valuation firms, where he focuses his new business development nationally. A graduate of Stanford University (AB, 1980) and Harvard Business School (MBA, 1984), Doug has a broad background in investment banking and venture capital. He has taught and written extensively on raising equity capital, valuations, and strategic planning.

From 1984 to 1993, he was an investment banker at Dean Witter Reynolds and Butcher & Singer (now First Union Wheat), closing over $3 billion of transactions, including public offerings, mergers and acquisitions, and private equity. From 1993 to 1996, he ran his own investment bank, Rogers Financial Group, focusing on mergers and acquisitions, venture capital financings, valuation, and due diligence. Since March 1996, Doug has focused on valuing high technology, biotechnology, and health care companies, assets and transactions.

How does an entrepreneur evaluate a business valuator?

When seeking financing, there are two basic ways to go: entrepreneurs can let prospective investors dictate the valuation or they can be more proactive, commissioning an independent valuation. When selecting a valuation firm, entrepreneurs should consider the following:

- Evaluate the valuation firm's client lists, client testimonies, and references that are related to the entrepreneur's business.
- Were the firm's valuations instrumental in raising capital?
- Does it understand my technology, niche, and intangibles?
- How attuned is it to my business plan?
- Does it appreciate where I fit into the market?
- Is it responsive and communicative?

How does a valuation firm value an Internet company?

There are a variety of valuation methodologies employed. Broadly speaking, we look at (1) the income or discounted cash flow, (2) the market or comparable companies, and (3) the cost approaches.

Under the income approach, we project the performance of the startup over a three-to-five–year period, discounting the projected cash flow at discount rates ranging from the teens to over 60%. The discount rate depends on a variety of factors, including the relative strength of the industry, the startup's financial capabilities, its resources, and the experience and reputation of management. In the final year of the projection period, we apply a capitalization rate to the final year's cash flow to reflect a realistic growth rate for the startup. The resulting discounted cash flow may be adjusted downward by a discount for lack of marketability (for private companies) or discount for lack of control (minority interest).

A related approach is employed by certain venture capitalists. Some venture capitalists focus on their expected holding period and, specifically, on the year of the VC's expected "exit" from the investment. Under this approach, the venture capitalist projects gross revenues for the year prior to the exit. If the startup cannot demonstrate the potential to generate revenues above the VC's minimum "hurdle" (minimum gross revenues), the venture capitalist may not have much interest. For example, some venture capitalists require $50 million in revenue in year 3 or 4 of the investment. If the startup can demonstrate such potential, the venture capitalists may then apply an industry price earnings ratio to the projected earnings in the final year before the exit in order to derive a future value for the company. To derive a present value for the company, the future value is discounted by the venture capitalist's target compounded rate of return. This will provide a "post-money" (after the VC's investment) valuation of the startup.

Under the market or comparable companies approach, there are two major analyses. The first looks at comparable transactions, including debt, equity, and mergers and acquisitions, completed for public and private companies similar to the startup in question. Revenue, income, or cash flow multiples are derived from this analysis, and adjustments are applied that may include a discount for lack of marketability (for private companies), discount for lack of control (for minority interests), or other adjustments reflecting differences between the startup company and the companies involved in those transactions. The second major analysis entails identifying and comparing public companies similar to the startup. This analysis involves deriving multiples (such as those just described) from comparable public companies, typically with an adjustment for lack of marketability (for private companies).

The cost approach entails an analysis of the costs required to replace the underlying assets of the startup. These assets may include its workforce, trademarks, copyrights, patents, key management, customer list, relationships, and other things. This approach focuses on the sum of the values of the individual tangible and intangible assets of the startup as a proxy for total enterprise value.

How much does it typically cost to have a company valued?

Typically, valuations cost from $5,000 to well over $40,000. That depends on the "turnaround time" of the engagement, the size and complexity of the startup, the profile of the transaction, the scrutiny (and associated risk) of the valuation, and so on.

How long does it take to have a company valued?

It varies. Typically, the low end is one week and the high end is four to five weeks depending on the availability of the valuation staff, the complexity of the startup, the availability of requested financial information from the company, the difficulty of finding comparable companies, the flexibility of the client's timetable, and other factors. For example, we might have to help construct from scratch a budget for the startup; this adds time to the process.

What roles do my accountant and attorney play in a valuation?

The accountants are often critical. The valuation firm will interface with the company's accountants to get financial information and get their view of the company's prospects.

Similarly, the lawyers will provide valuable legal information about the startup such as representatives and warranties, shareholder agreements, and any contingent liabilities.

In certain circumstances the valuation report may need to be signed off by the accountant or attorney. If it is a venture capital deal, the accountants and attorneys typically don't have to sign off. If the valuation provides the basis for stock option plans, then you need the startup's accountants to sign off because it might affect the value of the company. If the startup is involved in a merger or acquisition, then the startup's attorneys may need our fairness opinion for their transaction documents.

How does an entrepreneur use a valuation when negotiating with an investor?

How the entrepreneur uses the report depends on the sophistication and experience of the investor. Some investors will request that the entrepreneur get an independent valuation as a starting point for negotiations. However, a valuation can also provide an entrepreneur with the comfort, necessary education, and ammunition to deal with a sophisticated investor regardless of the investor's position on independent valuations.

What role does the valuation expert play in negotiating with an investor?

The valuation firm can be an excellent support for negotiating the venture transaction, merger, acquisition, or other transaction. An entrepreneur can "leverage" valuation advice to higher valuations. A good valuation firm will make a compelling case for the entrepreneur's perception of value and add to the entrepreneur's credibility.

Negotiating with investors is like walking through a minefield. I hope that the suggestions and anecdotes in this chapter will provide you with a guide on how to avoid getting blown up. Unfortunately, the winds of investment interest change quickly and, in most cases, in sync with the stock market. Therefore, a term sheet you get from an investor may be rescinded if what you are doing goes out of vogue. The only things you have control over in the process are your responses to the investor's questions.

CHAPTER SUMMARY

Every entrepreneur thinks he has reached the Promised Land when an investor offers a term sheet. Unfortunately, negotiating a term sheet is a very grueling process. To enhance your chances of striking a deal with an investor, remember to do the following:

- Hire a venture attorney.
- Anticipate issues and problems in advance and think through solutions.
- Listen to concerns with an open mind.
- Don't reply immediately to any question or issue; give each question a lot of thought before responding and run your responses by your advisors.
- Be flexible and remember you have to give something to get something.

Finally, determine if you really want to be in business with the investors you are negotiating with. If you are uncomfortable with the investors and you have options, consider them before agreeing to terms.

14

What Are Investors and Money Managers Interested in Investing In?

Every entrepreneur wants to know what private investors and venture capitalists are interested in investing in. It has been my experience that the only thing private investors and venture capitalists have in common is that they both want to see a substantial return on their money and would like to see their investments become liquid within five years.

PRIVATE INVESTOR INVESTMENT CRITERIA

The difference between the two is that private investors are willing to take more risk, usually have more business experience than venture capitalists, and typically invest in their areas of expertise. For example, I am in a venture called Worldfunding.com, an online portal for minority companies to find financing. The private investors who are interested in investing are all former bank presidents who know banks have a problem attracting enough quality loan applications. Raising money from individuals who understand and appreciate a particular market niche is easier than raising money from individuals or funds that are strictly opportunistic or focus on a particular area such as B2C, B2B, or software tools.

Robert E. Turner, 43, is chairman, chief investment officer, and founder of Turner Investment Partners, an employee-owned investment firm based in

Berwyn, Pennsylvania, with more than $10 billion in assets in stock, bond, and balanced accounts and mutual funds for institutions and individuals. Bob is the lead product manager of the Mercury Select Growth Fund, the Vanguard Growth Equity Fund, the Turner Technology Fund, and the Turner Top 20 Fund. He also serves as a co-manager of the Turner Midcap Growth Fund, the Turner B2B E-Commerce Fund, the Turner Global Top 40 Fund, and the Turner Wireless & Communications Fund, and covers the technology and producer-durables sectors for all Turner stock portfolios.

A chartered financial analyst, Bob previously served as a senior investment manager at Meridian Investment Company. He earned bachelor and MBA degrees at Bradley University.

I asked him to give us his views on what makes a compelling investment from private and institutional investors' points of view.

What areas of the Internet should an entrepreneur focus on?

The Internet infrastructure is what you should focus on. You want to be the weapon supplier. It's hard to determine who will be the winner. When Yahoo!, Infoseek, and Excite came out, no one knew who would dominate, but if you bought Yahoo! you did very well, and if you bought the others you did OK or fair. On the other hand, if you bought Cisco, Sun Micro, or EMC, which sell routers and other infrastructure technology, you have done incredibly well.

What do you look for in a management team?

Experience is really important. Successful startups have CEOs who have been out there before, either through having a senior position at an established company such as Oracle or having started and run other successful ventures that have gone public or have been sold to a public company.

I get nervous when I meet founders and wonder if they have the skills to build the business. A good founder knows her limitations and goes out and tries to recruit experienced people.

What is the future of the B2C sector?

The winners have already been established, such as Yahoo!, eBay, Amazon, and AOL. Anyone who tries to start a company in this area will not make it. The market isn't big enough for all of these niche players.

There are a lot of regional opportunities. Entrepreneurs can focus on building a company that can be bought by one of the big companies.

What is the future of the B2B sector?

The future is very big. Only a quarter of it will go to new companies. The rest will go to existing business that will be done through existing companies. The areas that entrepreneurs should focus on are the fragmented industries with no major gorillas. B2B is very complicated because everyone has different systems and software.

I think the IT services group such as Sapient Breakaway Solutions, Proxicom, and Scient have a lot of upside because they have the capability to connect the 100 moving parts.

What is the one piece of advice you would give today's Internet entrepreneurs?

You have to have a business that can scale. You have to be willing to execute that very quickly, which means you have to do a lot of acquisitions. It's like the life of a firefly—you glow and have your moment of glory. You need to be able to scale to build new products and develop strategic partnerships.

There are over 2,000 public companies in just the technology area. It's hard to keep investors' attention. Of the 400 public Internet companies, 5% have 80% of the value. Only one-third trade above the price they closed at the first day after going public. The message here is that for every successful Internet company, there are many, many failures.

VENTURE CAPITAL INVESTMENT CRITERIA

Professional venture capitalists primarily come from a banking or investment banking background. Some are former technologists and some have actual entrepreneurial and business operating experience. Venture capitalists have a lot of pressure to provide results in a short period of time. Most venture capitalists won't admit that they follow the investment interests of institutional money managers. What is important to a venture capitalist is not to build an enduring enterprise, but to invest in companies that have the chance to become substantial businesses and, more important, attract the interests of money managers such as Bob Turner.

If Bob Turner likes a concept and plans to invest in it, that gives the venture capitalist a chance to sell all or part of his investment and distribute the proceeds to his investors. This is why you see quick changes in investment interest by venture capitalists. A venture fund's customer is the money manager, and if the fund doesn't give the customer what he wants, then the customer can exit the investment.

Here is an interview with Harry Wallaesa, who is the president and chief operating officer of Safeguard Scientifics, Inc., one of the world's leading venture capital investors. Harry was also the founder, president, and CEO of aligne, Inc., a strategic technology management consulting firm. aligne, Inc., has helped a number of Safeguard partnership companies to improve their performance in addition to providing strategic management consulting services to executives of Fortune 500 companies.

Prior to founding aligne, Inc., Harry was the CIO and vice president of management information systems at Campbell Soup Company. In his 10 years at Campbell Soup, he made significant contributions to the company's resurgence as one of the top-performing companies in the food industry. Prior to joining Campbell Soup, Harry worked for IBM Corporation in various marketing positions.

In addition to his position at Safeguard, Harry is chairman of CompuCom Systems, aligne, Inc., and MegaSystems. He also serves as a director of the following boards: Redleaf Group LLC; The Pennsylvania Academy of Fine Arts; Bowne, Inc.; iMedium, Inc.; and the University of Pennsylvania Health Systems. Harry has a BS from Kutztown University.

What types of products should entrepreneurs focus on developing?

We are interested in Internet infrastructure. If I were an entrepreneur, I would focus on doing what I know. Go after an area you have a passion for. The areas we are interested in are telecommunications and software. If you can come up with a new business model that focuses on cost savings and innovation, those areas will probably gain acceptance.

What types of businesses were making the cut before, but aren't now?

Companies that don't show in their projections a future profit aren't going to find funding. Too many companies were focused on selling to

Wall Street. People called it the Gold Rush—and that is now in the past. People's prudence went by the wayside.

Business models that can't be differentiated and don't have significant barriers to entry and require tremendous amounts of capital to gain acceptance will have a hard time attracting funding. Today's business models have to have multiple revenue sources and must have the ability to drive significant earnings.

What types of entrepreneurs were making the cut before, but aren't now?

The types of entrepreneurs we invest in are confident, enthusiastic, and mature, and they understand how to build a great team. We will fund young entrepreneurs who have the maturity to attract seasoned profes-sionals to help build the business. Our view of the world hasn't changed in terms of what we invest in.

What is the best way for entrepreneurs to enhance their chances of getting funding?

They need to differentiate their business model and have good experi-ence in their industry. The market they are going after must be large enough, and they must be early to the game. In our particular case, we are a holding company, not a VC, so we are interested in synergies with the other companies in our partnership.

How many years of experience does an entrepreneur need in business to be taken seriously?

You don't have to have experience, but you need to attract people with experience to carry out your vision. Some of the best ideas we have seen have come from very young entrepreneurs who have surrounded them-selves with very experienced management.

Is having big-company experience a plus over entrepreneurial experience?

No! Business models are changing and are getting away from large-orga-nization bureaucracies. They are outsourced and driven by collaboration. They aren't built through vertically integrated high-cost structures and services. In a lot of cases large-company experience is a detriment and not a plus.

Coming from a large company can be a plus because of the business and training you receive. The key is not to lose flexibility and to continue to innovate. For me personally, working for a large company was a great experience. I wasn't typecast as a big-company guy. I learned a lot at IBM and Campbell Soup Company. What I learned a lot about was what not to do as opposed to what to do.

How important is having the right strategic partners?

It is really important. This is something we help entrepreneurs with. It's important for any business plan. It's good to have quality collaborators or partners. It shortens the time it takes to be successful. The days of exclusive arrangements are over, but it's good to get with partners that can help with the execution.

How important is it to have your management team lined up before you move in?

You don't have to have your entire team. We help entrepreneurs find the right people to build their companies. We have access to people that a lot of entrepreneurs don't have.

Should you recruit your own board members?

You should make a list of who you think would be good and then you should work with the venture capitalists to see who would be the best fit. Venture capitalists can assist in finding really terrific board members.

What is the one piece of advice you would give after being an entrepreneur and now a venture capitalist?

You need to demonstrate passion and confidence in your idea and be ready for a lot of hard work. Go and recruit the very best people you can because people make the business.

CHAPTER SUMMARY

Although this chapter gave you insights into what investors are interested in, don't get caught up in the latest investing fad. If you want to attract capital, focus on the following:

- *Niche.* Pick a local, national, or international opportunity that has a sizable, definable market with a minimum of competition. This means stay away from selling mass-market books, CDs, and electricity and focus on billion-dollar marketplaces such as supplying products to undertakers and county-government agencies.

- *Playing to your strengths.* Don't start an e-commerce business focused on a market that you have no knowledge of. If Jeff Bezos of Amazon, who had no book retailing experience, went to investors today with the same business plan that he used to raise money for Amazon, he wouldn't raise a dollar.

- *Management.* Recruit and hire knowledgeable, capable professionals who make investors whip out their checkbooks and beg you to take their money.

- *Right investors.* Don't waste your time sending your business plan for a construction online business exchange to pharmaceutical giant Glaxo-SmithKline's venture capital fund.

- *Business plan.* Develop an easy-to-read, well-thought-out business plan. The only entrepreneurs who receive investment without a business plan are entrepreneurs who made money for investors in the past. All the successful serial entrepreneurs I have worked with believe in and develop business plans.

Finally, if you are offered a term sheet, and the investors are people you respect and are comfortable with, don't be unreasonable. It's better to own 5% of a publicly traded company than 100% of an idea with no capital. If you have any questions, feel free to e-mail me at *marc@kramercommunications.com.*

SAMPLE BUSINESS PLAN

Worldfunding.com

"The Commerce Center for Minority Businesses"

TABLE OF CONTENTS

EXECUTIVE SUMMARY

Problem

The five minority business groups, as classified by the Bureau of the Census and Small Business Administration, are African American, Asian American, Indian, Hispanic, and Native American Indian. Currently, there is no online financial/business exchange for minority business executives to:

- Raise capital to start and run a business
- Buy and sell exclusively to minority businesses
- Find minority service providers
- Buy and sell services/products to each other

According to the Federal Reserve, every bank has Community Reinvestment Act (CRA) requirements to meet. Banks by law are required to lend a percentage of dollars equal to the percentage of dollars in their banking region.

Minority-owned companies that focus on getting contracts from Fortune 1000 companies and government entities must sell their businesses to another minority owner who will maintain a 30% or greater interest in the company to qualify as a minority-owned business. If they don't sell their business to another minority, they lose their contracts and the company loses a lot of its value.

According to Bill Larson, director of minority purchasing for Ford Motor Company ($8 billion a year with minority vendors) and a member of the Detroit Chapter of the National Minority Supplier Development Council (NMSDC), there is no destination website for minority companies to find funding. The NMSDC network includes a national office in New York and 39 regional councils across the country and certifies 15,000 minority businesses for its 3,500 corporate members whose minority purchases exceeded $41 billion in one year.

Facts:

- Minority-owned businesses represent only 11% of total businesses, 6% of gross receipts, and 3 to 4% of total corporate purchases.
- Twenty percent is the growth rate of minority businesses, according to the Small Business Administration.
- Minority firms generate $500 billion in revenue per year, according to the U.S. Bureau of the Census.

- There are over 1 million minority-owned businesses in the United States.
- According to the U.S. Bureau of the Census, 3,000 African-American businesses have $1 million or more in sales.
- According to the U.S. Bureau of the Census, 9,200 Hispanic-American businesses have $1 million or more in sales.
- According to the U.S. Bureau of the Census, 12,517 Asian-American businesses have $1 million or more in sales.

Company Description

Worldfunding.com is the first business exchange to assist minorities in:

- Finding capital (banking, factoring, and government, private, and institutional capital)
- Finding potential buyers of their businesses
- Finding minority service providers to provide services and products
- Training their employees to improve productivity, thus increasing their chances of success

Competition

Currently no destination site provides minorities with access to private individuals and institutions that provide working capital or to an exchange to buy and sell businesses, products, and services. There are four major competitors in the area of assistance in finding financing: DataMerge.com, OffRoadCapital.com, VCapital.com, and Garage.com.

Categories	DataMerge	OffRoadCapital	VCapital	Garage	Worldfunding
Button for minority funding	N	N	Y	N	Y
Funding categories					
City government funding	N	N	N	N	Y
Commercial banking	N	N	N	N	Y
County funding	N	N	N	N	Y
Credit unions	N	N	N	N	Y
Factoring (funding)	Y	Y	Y	N	Y

Categories	DataMerge	OffRoadCapital	VCapital	Garage	Worldfunding
Federal funding	N	N	N	N	Y
Institutional capital	N	Y	Y	Y	Y
Investment banking	N	N	N	N	Y
Leasing	N	N	N	N	Y
Private capital	N	Y	Y	Y	Y
Savings and loans	N	N	N	N	Y
State funding	N	N	N	N	Y
Venture capital	N	Y	Y	Y	Y
Businesses for sale					
Business-to-business	N	N	N	N	Y
Business-to-consumer	N	N	N	N	Y
Support services					
Accounting	N	N	Y	Y	Y
Board members	N	Y	N	N	Y
Business plan	N	Y	Y	Y	Y
Employment opportunities	N	N	Y	Y	Y
Executive coaching	N	N	N	Y	Y
Legal	N	N	Y	Y	Y
Marketing	N	N	Y	N	Y
Online training	N	N	N	N	Y
Sales	N	N	Y	N	Y

Competitive Advantages

- Worldfunding.com was the first to market with a dedicated B2B site for minority entrepreneurs to raise capital and business and sell businesses.
- Worldfunding.com is narrowly focused.
- Its management team has strong regional and national contacts.
- We have the largest and most comprehensive database of minority-owned businesses.

Marketing

Our marketing will be targeting two groups:

Group A: Presidents, vice presidents of sales and marketing, CFOs, and minority purchasing managers, banks, venture capitalists, factoring companies, and accounting, law, and investment banking firms.

Group B: Nonprofit chamber and trade association leaders, government officials, economic development organizations, media, and university business schools.

Our primary use of marketing dollars will be for direct mail, broadcast permission e-mail, print advertising, trade shows, and public relations.

Management

The management team has over 150 years of business operations and marketing experience.

- Chairman: The Honorable Tom Carter, former assistant secretary of commerce for economic development, U.S. Department of Commerce, during the Reagan administration
- Vice chairman: Ben Strauss, former chairman/CEO of American Bank, a $2 billion-in-asset regional bank in Philadelphia
- Vice chairman: Dilip Limaye, president/CEO of Ecom-Energy
- Board member: Thad Fortin, president of Haas Corporation, one of the leading outsource chemical management service firms in the United States
- President/CEO—Marc Kramer, former president of Mixed Media Works, which was acquired by US Interactives and ran seven startups and four turnarounds
- Vice president of banking relationships: Jean Fields, 19 years of commercial banking and employee training experience
- Chief marketing officer: Karen Barrett, 25 years of financial marketing experience
- CIO: Randy Feldman, 15 years of management information experience and currently the CIO of ECRI, a 300-person medical device testing company with offices worldwide.

- Vice president of content: Gail Jones, over 20 years of editorial experience with companies such as The Vanguard Group and AstraZeneca

We are in the process of recruiting minorities to the board of directors and will recruit minorities for key management positions. Service such as advertising, executive recruiting, marketing, website development, and hosting will be outsourced to minority-owned companies.

Sales Process

To support our marketing effort, we will have one salesperson per each minority group in each of the top eight cities in the United States. Those salespeople will be heavily involved with the ethnic group they are working with. We will launch in New York, Philadelphia, Miami, and Los Angeles in our first year.

Revenue

Years	Yr1	Yr2	Yr3	Yr4	Yr5
Revenue					
Placement fees	$312,500	$1,800,000	$5,184,000	$14,929,920	$32,248,627
Business sales	$ –	$2,750,000	$6,050,000	$13,310,000	$29,282,000
Business sales listing fee	$ –	$600,000	$990,000	$1,633,500	$2,695,275
Online training	$280,000	$1,108,800	$4,024,944	$14,610,547	$53,036,285
Books	$280,000	$616,000	$1,355,200	$2,981,440	$6,559,168
Employment opportunities	$252,000	$609,840	$1,475,813	$3,571,467	$8,642,950
Conferences	$ –	$1,320,000	$3,267,000	$8,085,825	$20,012,417
Service fees	$870,000	$1,914,000	$4,210,800	$9,263,760	$20,380,272
Sponsorship	$144,000	$316,800	$696,960	$1,533,312	$3,373,286
Total	$2,138,500	$11,035,440	$27,254,717	$69,919,771	$176,230,280
Total expenses	$3,883,172	$11,579,248	$22,677,226	$49,764,606	$121,384,005
Pretax profit/loss	$(1,744,672)	$(543,808)	$4,577,491	$20,155,165	$54,846,275

Worldfunding.com has nine sources of revenue. None of its revenue sources require the company to build distribution centers and take possession of products.

Capital Needs

Worldfunding.com is looking for $5 million in startup capital. We have corporate and private commitments totaling $750,000.

Exit Strategy

We believe this company has a tremendous chance to be successful and reach an IPO because of its niche and current competition.

OBJECTIVES

Objectives for two groups of years are as follows:

Years 1–2:

- Financial transactions—over 700 in the first two years: members (a minimum of four users per corporation)
- Public members—100 members (a minimum of four users per institution)
- Revenue—nearly $10 million by Year 2

Years 3–5:

- Financial transactions—over 6,000 by Year 5
- Year 3—profitable
- Revenue—over $170 million by Year 5
- Profits—40% plus pretax profit margins

MARKET

Small Business Usage

The number of small businesses with a Web presence has nearly doubled since 1998, and the coming years will see an even more dramatic increase, according to a nationwide survey of companies with fewer than 100 employees by International Communications Research commissioned by Prodigy Biz Corp., a subsidiary of Prodigy Communications Corp.

The research found that approximately one-third of small businesses currently have a Web presence. Research by International Data Corp. (IDC) found that 19% of small businesses were online one year ago. The Prodigy study also found that 40% more small businesses (approximately 2.1 million) without websites expect to be on the Internet within an average of the next eight months.

Despite perceived geographic barriers, 90% of small businesses anticipate benefiting from the Internet. When asked how the Internet would be used, small business respondents said their primary uses would be promoting to prospects (69%), followed by e-commerce (57%) and providing better customer service (48%). Other top responses included competing with other businesses (46%) and communicating with employees (11%). Nearly 75% of small business owners claim cost is not a barrier to setting up a website.

Forty-four percent of small business owners claim they do not have enough staff for, and 41% report they do not have time to, maintain a website. Overall, the study showed that the likelihood of having an Internet presence declines significantly with the overall size of the company. Only 25% of companies with fewer than 10 employees have an Internet presence. By contrast, half of those with 10 or more employees have taken advantage of this opportunity.

"Small businesses no longer have to spend hours toiling over their site design and updates," said Rick Miller, senior analyst of Internet strategies at Cahners In-Stat. "A website will be mandatory for any business in the twenty-first century, no matter what its size."

Primary Market

The NMSDC Network, which includes 39 affiliated regional councils, matches more than 15,000 certified minority-owned businesses (African American, Hispanic, Asian, and Native American) with its more than 3,500 corporate members, including America's top publicly owned, privately owned, and foreign-owned companies, as well as universities, hospitals, and other major buying institutions.

Minorities represent 26% of the population of the United States, but minority businesses represent only 11% of total businesses, 6% of gross receipts, and 3 to 4% of total corporate purchases.

The percentage of minorities online, according to Cyber Dialogue, is

- African Americans, 35%
- Asians, 7%
- Hispanics, 25%
- Indians, 45%
- Native American Indians, 30%

Market Interviews

We interviewed the following minority purchasing managers to see if there was a need for a minority vendor website:

- Karl Brockenborough, vice president for financial affairs for Cheyney University
- Bill Larson, purchasing manager for Ford Motor Company and board member of the Detroit chapter of the National Minority Supplier Development Council
- Ramon Moya, director of minority purchasing for Bell Atlantic
- Bill Pebble, purchasing manager for ADC Telecommunications

Through interviews, we have learned the following:

- There is no online or offline source for minority-owned businesses to find all the sources that will provide financing to minority-owned businesses.
- There is no website where corporations can go to find detailed information on minority vendors, although plans to put the NMSDC database online are being discussed. That database, according to those we interviewed, only provides names and contact information for certified companies. It does not provide detailed information about their revenue, past clients, or references.
- There is no website that aggregates minority opportunities.
- There is no website that provides minority-owned businesses a way to find other minority-owned businesses with which to partner and with which to buy and sell products and services.

REVENUE STREAMS

Worldfunding.com will have nine sources of revenue.

Placement fees: We will develop an investment capital matching service that will match minority-owned companies looking for capital with private investors, venture capitalists, investment banks, and commercial banks. We will have an agreement among Worldfunding.com and participating companies that want financing and investment banking firms that might handle certain transactions. We will charge 50 basis points for capital raised. Fifty percent will be taken in capital stock on a case-by-case basis and 50% in cash. In most cases the banks will pay the fee directly to Worldfunding.com.

Business sales: We will partner with a business broker to offer this service. We will share a 10% commission with a national business brokerage company.

Business listing fee: Companies will be able to list their businesses for sale. We will charge them $1,200 a year to list their companies.

Contract opportunities: We will offer members the opportunity to enter proposals and respond to proposals. Each vendor will sign a contract with Worldfunding.com to pay 10% of each consulting opportunity as a marketing fee.

Online training: We will enter into strategic alliances with accredited universities, training companies, and consultants to offer business training and seminars. We will charge our partner a 10% commission on gross sales.

Conferences: We will list conferences (trade associations and business and convention bureaus) and provide online processing capabilities. We will list conferences for $500 and charge 5% commission to the conference for each person who signs up through our service.

Bookstore: We will offer books through a partnership with Amazon. The books will be selected by and for culture and demographics. We will earn a 10% gross commission on each book sold.

Employment recruiting: We will offer a service that allows companies that want to recruit minority students and professionals to advertise for them on our website. We will charge a placement fee of $100 and 5% commission on people who are hired.

Sponsorship: Companies will be able to sponsor sections and run banner advertisements that will link to their websites or to their corporate information on Worldfunding.com's website or to a specific offer. The average sponsorship will cost $2,000 a month.

CONTENT DESCRIPTION

According to interviews with Lycos and Excite search engine managers, the way we have constructed the website content should put us at the top of any minority vendor or minority business search conducted that relies on a combination of the following:

- Title tags
- Meta tags
- Human editors
- Links to our site

The website includes the following sections:

Company: There will be background information on the company and names and contact information for sales, customer service, and editorial.

Membership: There will be a one-page description of each member. Companies that decide to become members will fill out an online form that provides the following:

- Name
- Address
- Telephone
- Fax
- E-mail address
- Website address
- Top corporate officers' names
- Revenue size
- Client references
- Certifications

Investment capital: We will provide minority companies with access to bankers, private investors, venture capitalists, and investment bankers. Companies will put in what type of capital needs they have and what structure they would like the investment to be. Using rfpMarket.com software, we will send those leads to interested financial parties.

Business for sale: We will describe businesses without providing names. The companies for sale will be broken down by category. At a higher level we will eventually get involved in mergers and acquisitions.

Minority vendor categories: Purchasing departments and corporate management will be able to access a password-protected database that will allow them to find the type of vendor they want by size, years of experience, qualifications, clients, and geography using SIC and Product Service codes.

Contract opportunities: Companies will be able to post vendor needs, and we will use software developed by rfpMarket.com that sends proposals to companies tagged in our database that are interested in specific opportunities. For example, if a company is looking for a website, the proposal will be sent only to Web developers.

Online training: We will partner with a major business university such as the Wharton School and offer online distance learning in the following disciplines:

- Human resources
- Management
- Marketing
- Sales

Books/tapes: We will partner with Amazon to offer books specifically targeted to small-to-medium-sized businesses and will select books focused on minority business interests in the following areas:

- Capital formation
- Computers
- Customer service
- Leadership
- Management
- Marketing

- Motivation
- Public relations
- Sales

Employment opportunities: We will partner with an online minority-recruiting firm such as Minorityjobsbank or Minorityrecruiter to assist members in finding employees for the following types of positions:

- Accounting
- Advertising
- Computer sciences
- Engineering
- Human resources
- Legal
- Marketing
- Public relations
- Software development
- Websites

Business news: We will provide news on minority-owned businesses that span various minority groups. There will be six types of business news/interviews that we will provide:

- CEO interviews: Each week we will interview a different CEO about the challenges and opportunities he or she is dealing with.
- Company/news: We will post press releases of all of our members on a daily basis similar to what Venturewire.com does.
- Human resources: We will have human resource professionals, executive recruiters, and compensation specialists write and be interviewed about recruiting and retaining personnel.
- Financial: We will have investment bankers, venture capitalists, and bankers write and be interviewed about how to finance companies.
- Marketing: We will have marketing professionals write and be interviewed about marketing and branding strategies.
- Sales: We will have sales professionals write and be interviewed about sales.

Events: There are regional, national, and minority-focused business events. We will work with event planners and list events and take enrollment online. We will store the users' contact information, so the next time they decide to go to an event they won't have to type in their contact information. They will only have to enter a credit card number.

MARKETING SITE

Marketing for our site is not very complicated because we have specific target users of the site. Our strategy includes all forms of marketing, except television and radio.

Target Users

- *Minority vendors:* We will buy mailing lists that contain names of presidents, vice presidents of marketing, vice presidents of sales, and salespeople.
- *Private sector:* We will target minority purchasing managers and minority human resource recruiters, and minority and nonminority accounting, banking, legal, investment banking, marketing, advertising, and product-oriented companies.
- *Public sector:* We will target minority purchasing managers for local, state, and federal governments, school districts, and colleges and universities.
- *Students:* We will target business, computer science, science, marketing, and English undergraduates and graduate students.
- *Trade associations and chambers:* We will join, sponsor, and make mailings to national and regional trade associations/chamber leaders and their members.

Building Visibility Tools

- *Direct mail:* We will buy traditional mailing lists and e-mail publications.
- *Direct e-mail:* We will purchase a permission mailing list from Bigfoot.com, one of the leading direct e-mail companies in the United States. A permission marketing list is a list of e-mail addresses of individuals who are interested in receiving information by e-mail on topics that interest them.

- *Print advertising:* We will run quarter-page advertisements in newspapers such as *The Philadelphia Tribune, Asian News,* and *Hispanic News* and third-of-a-page advertisements in publications such as *Black Entrepreneur and Purchasing Manager Today* and with the National Council of Minority Suppliers. We will also look at purchasing advertisements in national magazines such as *The Wall Street Journal, USA Today, Business Week, Forbes,* and *Fortune* by region.

- *Public relations:* We will send press releases to minority publications, radio and television stations, and targeted public- and private-sector members.

- *Partner promotion:* We will work with our sponsors and business partners to send out direct mail pieces and to have links from their websites to our site.

- *Affiliate programs:* We will develop relationships with minority-oriented chambers of commerce and trade associations to promote the site in return for revenue that is derived from those who enter our site through their websites.

- *Events:* We will run events with chambers of commerce and trade associations to promote the site and we will attend trade shows sponsored by these partners.

SALES

Our sales strategy is multifaceted. Our product and service offerings from sponsorships to sales partnerships to memberships. Therefore, we will implement a variety of sales tactics.

Memberships: In order to develop a large user group and community of interest, we will give membership away for free for at least one year and consider charging a subscription fee after we see how customers are using the site.

Sponsorship sales: We will have a team of experienced advertising salespeople, who will come from minority publications, to sell sponsorship and banner advertising. Banks and insurance agencies have targeted budgets to promote products to minority companies.

New product show sales: We will hire people with Fortune 500 sales experience and large contact databases to encourage companies to promote their products through our site.

Contract opportunities: We will send out broadcast e-mail pieces and link people to the section of the site that will allow them to enter proposals and respond to proposals. We will limit and screen the number of service providers and charge them an annual fee plus a percentage of each proposal that they win.

Online training: We will send direct mail and e-mail to promote our educational offerings, and then allow our partners to handle sales leads.

Surveys: We will send direct mail and e-mail to promote our in-house surveys and we will have salespeople responsible for contacting companies to promote our custom survey capabilities.

Books: We will do broadcast e-mail to promote our bookstore.

Travel: We will do broadcast e-mail to promote our travel program.

Employment opportunities: We will do broadcast e-mail to promote our Employment Opportunities section and allow our partners to take leads we receive and convert them into sales.

Events: We will have salespeople who contact trade associations, chambers of commerce, and companies to promote their events through our membership and encourage members to sign up for events online.

RETENTION

Our long-term success will be based on our ability to retain users. We have a retention plan for each target group:

Members

In order to encourage buyers to submit requests, we plan to do the following:

Management interface: Worldfunding.com has built a management interface to help users easily manage contacting and rejecting vendors, making sure that users have a positive experience.

Follow-up phone calls: We will follow up with a percentage of our users to make sure that they are satisfied.

Focus groups: We will conduct focus groups each quarter to stay in contact with buyers and to find out how we can improve our service.

Sweepstakes: Each month we will give away a one-week vacation. Each time a buyer enters a request, he or she will have an additional chance to win. For example, someone who enters six requests in a month will have six chances to win in that particular month.

Market research: We will provide buyers with information about what products and services are most bought through our service and give the range and average of those prices. We will also provide members with monthly statistics on traffic, advertising, and revenue earned.

Advisory board: We will create an advisory board made up of 12 of our users. This group will be charged with advising on how to improve our content and services and what new services and categories we should be adding. The board will be changed every two years.

Ongoing analysis: We will provide ongoing analysis and feedback to help members earn more revenue.

Users

Focus on requests: Management believes that to retain users we need to make it easy for companies seeking capital to apply for it. We also need to make sure we supply the companies providing capital with the appropriate information; therefore, we need to involve them in the design of the application.

Education: We try to educate vendors to help them focus their efforts and write good replies.

Focus groups: We will conduct semiannual online and offline focus groups to determine how we can improve the process.

Winner information: We will post information on which companies had won contracts. Vendors need to know that the system works.

COMPETITION

There are four potential competitors. None of the competitors are focused on minority businesses. As you saw in the spreadsheet in the executive summary, none focus on the following:

- Local, state, and county funding
- Access to service providers
- Providing a forum to buy and sell businesses

Garage.com

Mission: Garage.com helps entrepreneurs and investors build great businesses. This website claims to differ from typical venture capital firms that raise money from external sources and then invest the funds in various investment opportunities. At Garage.com, conversely, each member investor makes an independent investment decision and each entrepreneur chooses the investor with whom he wishes to partner.

The funds are transferred directly from the investor to the entrepreneur, and the two parties negotiate valuation, equity investment, and operational participation, without the involvement of Garage.com. Rather than compete with venture capital firms, this website helps them get together with startup companies. Also, since the average Garage.com entrepreneur is a startup business seeking from $1 million to $2 million in seed funding, venture capital firms are not usually interested in these opportunities. Garage.com finds "angels" for these average entrepreneurs. The targeted users of this website are both entrepreneurs seeking seed-level money and independent investors seeking to become involved with this type of startup business. The message to the targeted user is relatively simple: This is the place to find the "angels" needed to get startup businesses off the ground.

Functionality: This website is very easy to navigate. The homepage is arranged with a menu at the top of the page and the same links, in large print, in the center of the page. The links include the following:

- "Start Here"—learn what this site can do for the user.
- "Forums"—gain valuable insights through focused articles and Q&As from business experts.
- "Newsroom"—browse stories, opinions, and articles of interest to high-tech investors and entrepreneurs.

- "Garage"—find valuable resources to build businesses (for entrepreneurs).
- "Resources"—get valuable information and assistance on startup-related issues.
- "Startup Jobs"—look for select jobs in the high-tech industry.
- "Bootcamp"—learn the fundamentals of taking a company from startup to IPO in this two-day seminar.

There are small banner advertisements for the site sponsors near the bottom of the page along with the site's disclosure statement. There are two links at the bottom of the page, "Contact Us" and "Privacy Policy." The transition from page to page is fast without any delays. Many of the areas are repetitive, and there are areas available only to members. No special programming or software is required to use this website, and everything appears to function as designed.

User Benefit: The goal of Garage.com is to benefit two groups of users: entrepreneurs and investors. Assisting entrepreneurs in obtaining seed-level financing is the primary objective of this website. Garage.com strives to compress the entrepreneurs' "time-to-money" via mentoring and a high-quality investment network, allowing them to focus more time on building their businesses. This site also provides member entrepreneurs with expert advice, research and reference materials, and topical forums to help them launch and grow their startup businesses. For investors, Garage.com will identify and provide prescreened, high-quality investment opportunities that match the individual investor's identified areas of interest. All information is presented in a standard format to help investors analyze and evaluate companies quickly. Additionally, member investors have access to a broad community of investors focused on the cutting edge of high technology, enabling them to work together as they identify and qualify investment opportunities.

Owner Benefit: When a company is accepted into the Garage.com portfolio, the company compensates Garage.com, through a broker/dealer, after the company receives funding. The broker/dealer receives a small percentage of the new money raised. Investors are charged an annual membership fee. Both member companies and investors are given a 90-day, free, no-obligation trial. Garage.com also has small banner advertisements on several of the pages, providing another revenue stream.

Strengths/Weaknesses: Garage.com's objective is to bring startup businesses together with investors interested in these types of companies. This site is able to differentiate itself from other venture capital sites by focusing on seed-level companies. The functionality of this website is much more logical and the site is easier to use than the other sites reviewed. The "bootcamp" feature is unique and could prove to be very useful to beginners in these areas of interest. A cost to entrepreneurs and investors is mentioned but not specified. The site presents a great deal of information arranged to make access easy, but there is quite a bit of repetition. The forums provide useful information but also function as vehicles for advertisements.

VCapital.com

Mission: VCapital.com was developed in response to the perceived need of businesses to raise capital. This website was designed by venture capitalists and capital-backed entrepreneurs who understand the frustrations of raising capital. The founders and operators of this site have been on the "other side." They started out looking for capital and know what it's like to be turned down or just ignored. The VCapital.com network consists of leading professional venture capital providers and professional service providers. The founding venture capitalists represent a diverse cross section of the venture capital community, consisting of law firms, accounting firms, and others experienced in this arena. The goal of this website is to assist the businesses in searching for the right venture capitalists, preparing an appropriate presentation, providing advice in an honest and timely manner, and providing referrals to targeted venture capitalists. The targeted users of this website are business owners looking for capital to improve or expand their businesses. There are also opportunities for capitalists searching for the appropriate vehicle in which to invest. The message to targeted users is that this is the place to find the assistance they need to connect with venture capitalists ready to supply the funds needed to take their business to the next level.

Functionality: This website is set up to present information on VCapital.com in a way that is logical and makes it easy to find the desired areas of the site. Menus are set up at the top of the page and down the left margin. These menus provide links to the different areas of the site, including how VCapital.com works, introductions to the individual venture capitalists, an area to ask questions of the experts, the various communities, professional services, the "istore," and industry news. The vertical menu presents links to a site search engine, site map, the different types of information on the site, and the individuals involved with VCapital.com. The home page contains much press release/marketing information along with a number of advertisements. A great deal of information is presented on this website, spread out over many pages. The pages on the site are easy to access and move between, and the site functions quickly. The site map presents all the links and is the easiest way to navigate VCapital.com. The whole site works like a large database of information that the user cannot interact with or sort. This site simply presents the information on VCapital.com and provides an area to request information or assistance from the professional capitalists involved with it.

User Benefit: VCapital.com is a website devoted to bringing business owners looking for venture capital together with the professional venture capitalists who can help them. The targeted users of this website benefit through the use of the services provided. The first step is the search function that helps entrepreneurs determine which venture capitalists to target. The search is followed by assistance with their business plan presentation. In addition to assisting with business plan presentation, the professionals also review the information in the plan and provide honest and timely feedback. The final step in this process is submitting the business plan to venture capitalists. The professionals at VCapital.com use their connections with others in the industry to get the business plan reviewed instead of just added to the pile. This site also offers information and assistance with business-related issues, such as human resources, marketing, and sales.

Owner Benefit: The owners of this website benefit in a number of ways. The first is by introducing venture capital professionals and service providers to opportunities associated with businesses looking for assistance. Several revenue streams are available to VCapital.com. The most obvious of these are from advertising and from charging commissions on deals consummated through the website. The success or failure of this site should be relatively easy to determine. If VCapital.com is able to deliver venture capitalists willing to provide the needed money at competitive costs to the business owner, users will continue to come here for the assistance they need.

Strengths/Weaknesses: VCapital.com offers a large quantity of information that is logically arranged and easy to access. In addition to providing access to professional venture capitalists looking for good investment opportunities, this site offers advice on business plan content and presentation, followed by referrals to venture capitalists. Advertising is used to raise revenues and a commission is charged to connect the business owner to the capital providers. While there is much information on this website, it is spread over many pages and quite a few of the links are repetitive. Financial charges to the site users are not very well explained, and the commission fees are not easy to find.

DataMerge.com

Mission: DataMerge.com provides financing sources and financing "how to" programs to business owners, commercial real estate finance professionals, and finance consultants, both within the United States and internationally. This website began as a proprietary in-house databank for a Denver law firm. The company CEO saw an opportunity to market this database to other businesses and the public to allow access to the alternative funding sources the firm had developed over time. Since its startup, DataMerge.com has grown from simply offering its database to marketing a complete line of business financing tools. DataMerge.com sells all its products through its home office in Denver. Customers buy direct by telephone. Other distribution methods include cross-marketing programs with trade associations and software publishers to sell their products, and individual dealer agreements. The message to the targeted users is that DataMerge.com is offering the expertise and access to funding that the user needs, and this is the best place to meet those needs.

Functionality: This is a difficult site to use. Most of the pages use frames. These frames move independently and the control bars take up a lot of room on the screen. Some of the frames on the home page overlap and there is no way to see all of the information presented. A menu in the upper left frame includes links to "Financing Resources," "Who Is DataMerge?" "Financing News," "Find a Lender," "Success Stories," and "Join Our Database." The center of the home page allows electronic submission of loan application information for commercial real estate. There are also short blurbs on the products offered on this website. A table presenting DataMerge.com products is organized into three columns: product name, type, and description. Once the user gets past the pages with frames, the site functions quickly when switching pages and presenting different pages of information. There is no specialized programming or software required. Basically, this website is an advertisement for DataMerge rather than an actual forum for conducting business.

User Benefit: User benefits have to be separated into two categories. The first is benefits from using the products developed and marketed by DataMerge. The second is the benefits from using the DataMerge.com website.

DataMerge presents a number of business financing tools. The most important of these products is the Financing Sources Databank. This database features thousands of active financiers across the country, allowing business people to reach beyond their local contacts and geographic barriers in their search for capital. A second product is a manual and software program on raising capital through SCOR (Small Corporate Offering Registration). There are several other software programs available, each dealing with topics relating to business development. These include business plan guides, cash flow analyzers, mortgage planners, marketing kits, and so on. The benefit of the actual website is mostly limited to reviewing information on the products offered and the company itself. An area on the home page leads the user to expect selected portions of the venture capital database, based on project facts submitted from the site, to be available over the Internet.

Owner Benefit: This website serves as an advertisement for DataMerge. It presents information related to the company and its products in an easy-to-understand format. DataMerge.com appears to have taken a first, small step in putting some of its products online with the offering of sections of its venture capital database to interested users. There is no advertising apparent on DataMerge.com and, as the products aren't sold online, no direct revenue stream from the website. With Internet use growing at a rapid pace, even a website devoted to simply presenting information on the products and company is a valuable forum for getting news on the company out to the targeted users.

Strengths/Weaknesses: This website presents information on DataMerge in a direct manner that is easy to understand and use. The owners of the site have begun experimenting with online transactions in addition to the marketing efforts already well established on the site. One weakness is that the products aren't available online. Although a contact is given to order the products by telephone, costs are not provided on the website. A final drawback is the use of frames on the home page. The frames are not centered correctly and some information is obscured by overlaps.

OffRoadCapital.com

Mission: "Log in to OffRoadCapital's private capital marketplace—and invest in companies while they're still private." OffRoadCapital.com is a financial services company that uses the Internet to create a private capital marketplace. By combining the discipline of the public stock market with the efficiency and global reach of online technology, OffRoadCapital.com brings together high-net-worth individuals wanting access to private equity investment opportunities with established, privately owned companies that need financing in the $3 million to $15 million range. OffRoadCapital.com is in the business of arranging equity capital for companies seeking to grow through internal expansion, pursue an acquisition, recapitalize a balance sheet, or facilitate an ownership transition, including management buyouts. This website targets three audiences: individual investors, financial advisors, and businesses. The message to these targets is that OffRoadCapital.com is the place to find the funding in this difficult capital range because it is a level that doesn't attract the attention of traditional investment banks. A second reason to use this website is that OffRoadCapital.com has a captive, widely distributed network of investors ready to participate in private equity investment opportunities.

Functionality: OffRoadCapital.com contains a lot of information. This website doesn't have the large number of pages that some of its competitors do, but there is still repetition with some of the links. The home page for this website is very simple. There is a menu at the top of the page with links to "About OffRoadCapital," "Services," "FAQs," "Privacy," "Press," and "Contact OffRoadCapital." A little bit of information is summarized on this page and each summary links to another section of the site. There are also links to join the site and for members to log in. The "OffRoadCapital teams with" section presents small banners for teaming partners. These banners appear to function as small advertisements for the teaming partner. The transition from page to page is fast and no special programming or software is required. Many of the links take the user to the same place over and over again as they search for specific information.

User Benefit: Prior to the creation of private capital marketplaces, financing in the $3 million to $15 million range was difficult to obtain, and access to private equity investment opportunities was scarce. OffRoadCapital.com brings together business owners and investors in an efficient, orderly, and controlled marketplace. This website claims its marketplace is characterized by several significant innovations:

- Standardized online ordering mechanisms that present information in a consistent format for easy evaluation and comparison.
- An "OffRoadCapital Show" for each investment opportunity, which supports the free flow of information between company principals and investors through a series of interactive online meetings and e-mail exchanges.

- Market pricing of securities, based on the level of interest expressed by investors after performing their own due diligence.

- Standardized terms and conditions for each of the five available deal structures.

- Mandated quarterly and annual performance reporting throughout the life of the investment.

OffRoadCapital.com functions as a financial intermediary for the business owner and the investor. Its assistance is arranged into six distinct phases:

1. Assessing the business's needs

2. Understanding the business

3. Preparing the offering

4. Building investor interest

5. Closing the transaction

6. Providing ongoing support

Owner Benefit: The purpose of OffRoadCapital.com is to bring together businesses looking for funding and investors looking for private equity investment opportunities. The owners of the site do much more than just bring the two parties together and most likely realize some financial reward for their efforts. The percentage or fee charged could not be located on the website. Another potential revenue stream is the small advertising banners for the site's teaming partners. OffRoadCapital claims to be able to produce investors in the $3 million to $5 million range.

Strengths/Weaknesses: The strength of OffRoadCapital.com is that it is very easy to understand what it is trying to accomplish. The site is looking for business owners and investors in a very specific niche, one in which it is difficult to find funding. If, as the site claims, mainstream financial vehicles overlook this level of funding, users should be lining up to join this site. The most glaring weakness of OffRoadCapital.com is that it doesn't explain the ways in which it benefits financially, meaning the basis or amount of its fee is not discussed. Additionally, there doesn't appear to be any way to conduct these transactions online, which reduces this website to a simple advertisement.

Worldfunding.com's Competitive Advantage

We have nine competitive advantages:

1. We are first to market with our type of concept.

2. We are narrowly focused.

3. Our marketing professionals are minorities and have strong ties to their communities.

4. No one has a minority business database that is as extensive as ours.

5. We have business relationships with prospective customers and strategic allies.

6. We have experience at running financial businesses.

7. Our vision and strategic focus are more attuned to small companies.

8. We have access to substantial financial resources.

9. Our databases allow us to measure our effectiveness and make appropriate changes in our business model.

MANAGEMENT

Chairman: Honorable Tom Carter

Tom Carter currently operates a consulting business in Reston, Virginia, and serves on the board of directors of Resource America, Inc., and Pico Holdings, Inc. He also serves on the boards of directors of Retirement Street.Com and the Armed Forces Dental Benevolent Association as well as the board of advisors of Passport Health, Inc.

He has previously served on the board of directors of Dominion Bank; Graphic Scanning, Inc.; Cataract, Inc.; Computer Dynamics, Inc.; SENSYS, Inc.; and numerous other corporations.

His clients have included Fortune 100 corporations and medium-size businesses. He is currently involved in the design and development of Internet-based businesses. He has provided services in management analysis, compensation, international trade, finance, and strategic planning.

In 1981, he was appointed by President Ronald W. Reagan as the assistant secretary of commerce for economic development at the U.S. Department of Commerce. He served on the White House Urban Policy Task Force and the President's Council on Integrity and Efficiency, and as a member of the U.S. Department of the Treasury Task Force on Debt Management. He also held positions as the alternate U.S. executive director of the Inter-American Development Bank (1984–85) and special assistant and deputy assistant administrator for resource development of the U.S. Department of Housing and Urban Development (1969–72).

He has a BS from Michigan State University, a Master of City and Regional Planning from Catholic University, and a Diploma in Engineering Science from the U.S. Naval Post Graduate School. He also completed a seminar in Professional Public Management conducted by the Harvard Graduate School of Business and the Kennedy School of Government.

He is the author of *New Towns: Another Way to Live* (a 1976 Book-of-the-Month Club selection) and over 100 articles published in newspapers and magazines.

Vice Chairman: Ben Strauss

Ben is the founder of American Bank and served as the chairman and chief executive officer of American, Inc., for 25 years. American Bank, a publicly held company, recently merged with Arizona-based Wrangler Bank. At the time of the merger, American Bank was a $2 billion–asset commercial bank. Ben is currently chairman of United America as well as a board of director for Life Insurance. In addition to his extensive accomplishments as chairman of American Bank, Ben has won numerous awards for his outstanding leadership as well as many philanthropic awards.

Vice Chairman: Dilip Limaye

Dilip is an internationally recognized expert on energy issues, including deregulation of energy industries. He is the president and CEO of Ecom-Energy, a leading multinational energy research and consulting firm. Dilip was also the founder and president of the International Energy Services Company (INTESCO), the first multinational energy performance contracting company. He is an investor and partner in INTESCO Global Partners, LLC, a company that specializes in on-site generation and independent power production services to a wide range of industrial and commercial customers including health care facilities. He has published six books on energy-related topics and has presented more than 60 papers at major national and international conferences.

Board Member: Thad Fortin

Thad began his career in 1981 as operations manager with the Haas Corporation, a specialty chemical manufacturer in Philadelphia, Pennsylvania. In 1999, he was promoted to CEO. In 1985, Thad assumed sales responsibilities for the new midwest territory. Within three years, this territory became Haas's largest region. In 1988, Thad started Haas of Canada and Haas of Mexico. These companies represent more than 40% of total Haas sales.

In 1990, Thad was promoted to executive vice president, where his duties included complete responsibility for the automotive market. In 1996, Thad was named president of Haas Corporation. In this role, Thad is extremely active in all aspects of Haas's chemical management programs.

He also sits on the boards of two companies: Omnikem and Sun & Earth. Thad is a graduate of Ithaca College (BS, 1981).

President/CEO: Marc Kramer

Marc is a former partner at USWeb, the world's largest Internet consulting firm. Prior to that he was president of Mixed Media Works (MMW), an interactive company that produced websites for Rosenbluth International and CoreStates Bank, among others.

Before joining MMW, Marc started the Eastern Technology Council, the second-largest business technology council in the United States with over 1,000 corporate members. Marc has also served as interim president/CEO of *Business Philadelphia* and *Seven Arts,* two large regional magazines.

Marc has received such awards as the Inc. Magazine Entrepreneur of the Year and American Electronics Association Spirit of America Award. Three years in a row he was named one of the Top Five Business Leaders Under Age 40 in the Philadelphia region by the Philadelphia Jaycees.

Marc's first book, *Power Networking,* was published by the Tribune Company in the fall of 1997. His second book, *Small Business Turnaround,* published by Adams Media, came out in the fall of 1999.

He is a trustee of Cheyney University, the oldest African-American University in the United States. Marc has a master's degree in management from Pennsylvania State University and a BS in journalism from West Virginia University.

Vice President of Banking Relationships: Jean Fields

Jean was responsible for Community Reinvestment Act compliance for Jefferson Bank and oversight of CRA compliance for Jefferson Bank. She maintained the bank's "Satisfactory" rating through three examinations after upgrading it from a "Needs to Improve" rating.

Jean managed and expanded a portfolio of commercial loan relationships. She assists clients with all facets of the banking relationship by identifying client needs and recommending appropriate solutions. She also chaired the Government Lending Committee that developed and refined the bank's SBA lending process and procedures.

She now directs the business resource, information, and referral program. She has a BA from Indiana University of Pennsylvania, and studied French language and literature at L'Université de Nancy in Nancy, France.

Chief Marketing Officer: Karen Barrett

Karen is a former senior vice president and chief marketing officer for the consumer finance division of Enhance Financial Services Group (EFS). As CMO she developed the strategy and managed the marketing and operations for two of its Internet business sites. She also developed the Internet business plan and financial model for an additional Internet business. Development of this new site will be a joint venture between EFS and a database marketing Internet company. At EFS she managed several successful acquisitions. More recently, she developed the highly successful DRTV (direct response television) campaign with spokesperson Judge Joseph A. Wapner.

Before joining Enhance, Karen's 25-year career was focused in the financial services industry. She has held key marketing positions involving nontraditional, innovative credit, investment and asset-backed consumer and institutional products. She has managed the development and marketing for unique technology products and services for Bank One in Columbus, Ohio, including the two patented credit/debit card products. She also managed the development and implementation of its dial terminal authorization service using nontraditional communications providers.

As senior vice president of The Huntington Bank, she developed and managed its proprietary mutual fund family, growing assets from $200 million to $1 billion. Karen has extensive product development and marketing experience in all direct response and print media and in direct and indirect sales management. She has directed government relations and public relations in her marketing assignments. Karen has a BS in business from Ohio State University, where she has also done postgraduate work.

CIO: Randy Feldman

Randy directs all technology operations as CIO at ECRI, an international nonprofit corporation headquartered in Plymouth Meeting, Pennsylvania. Managing five service departments totaling over 50 personnel, he has designed and implemented a complete technology revolution within ECRI. The result was a 25% increase in its annual revenues to over $23 million in 1999. His management and continual hands-on work resulted in the recent completion of a new Internet presence, which promises to provide the basis for greater growth in its membership by offering Web access to its highly regarded services and publications.

A graduate of Bucknell University and Penn State University, Randy previously managed and supported the technical services at the Vanguard Group as their senior analyst and consultant. While at Vanguard, he led the transitions of most of its information technologies, the creation of its online services, and the support of its changing infrastructure. Before that, Randy was the network operations manager at US Healthcare during its peak growth years and when it became number one on the list of the fastest growing companies in the country.

Vice President of Content: Gail S. Jones

Gail has over 20 years of experience in publications management, marketing support, editing, and writing for a broad range of industries including pharmaceutical (AstraZeneca, L.P.), environmental (Roy F. Weston, Inc.), scientific (VWR Scientific Products), financial (The Vanguard Group), and computer-related (Aydin Computer Systems, Keystone Computer Associates, and Ketron, Inc.). She has performed report administration, document coordination, and information research.

Gail's strength is her knowledge, accuracy, and attention to detail. Her background of editing both promotional and technical copy gives her great flexibility and competence. Her BA is in communications from the University of Central Florida.

TECHNOLOGY

Objectives

- Automation of all components
- Scalable back office management
- Scalable website

Existing Technology

- Fully functioning website
- Application to import new vendors
- Application to manage RFPs/vendors
- Application to pre-register vendors
- Application to manage site traffic and event logging
- Simple partnering program implementation
- Banner ad back office management
- E-commerce linking implemented
- Tools and products used to build application
- Microsoft SQL server for database
- Internet Information Server (IIS) as web server with Front Page extensions
- Microsoft SMTP for CDONTS e-mailing
- Active Server Pages (ASP) for serving web pages and gluing to database
- Active Data Object (ADO) for executing queries against the database
- ASP containing embedded SQL for majority of the application with some stored procedures for making ADO calls to the database
- CyberCash for credit checking
- Visual InterDev for building the application
- Source Safe for source code control

Site Scalability

The following servers will help us scale the site as it grows:

- Two database servers with replication capabilities running on separate NT servers with four CPUs each
- Two IIS servers with load-balancing capabilities running on separate NT servers with four CPUs each
- One Microsoft Proxy Server on a separate NT Server
- ADO with connection pooling enabled for better database I/O
- MSMQ for bank wire instructions for processing and managing cash transactions

LAUNCH PLAN

Month	Action Item
1	Developing the content strategy and implementation plan for each city
1	Developing Worldfunding.com home page
1	Interviewing advertising/sales personnel
2	Interviewing advertising/sales personnel
2	Developing relationships with regional Worldfunding.com organizations
2	Developing home page for Worldfunding.com
2	Developing Worldfunding.com website
2	Interviewing editorial personnel
3	Developing Worldfunding.com website
3	Extending offers to advertising/sales personnel
3	Extending offers to editorial personnel
4	Developing the editorial content
4	Developing Worldfunding.com website
4	Preparing marketing materials and developing marketing plan
5	Approving marketing plan
6	Approaching advertising agencies and companies that buy direct
7	Promoting site through PR, direct e-mail, and direct mail

(continued)

Month	Action Item
7	Approaching advertising agencies and companies that buy direct
7	Signing 100 members a month
8	Promoting site through PR, direct e-mail, and direct mail
8	Signing 100 members a month
8	Closing on two to four advertisers
9	Closing on two to four advertisers
9	Promoting site through PR, direct e-mail, and direct mail
9	Signing 100 members a month
10	Closing on four to six advertisers
10	Signing 100 members a month
11	Closing on six to eight advertisers
11	Signing 100 members a month
12	Closing on six to eight advertisers
12	Signing 100 members a month

FINANCIALS

Years	Yr1	Yr2	Yr3	Yr4	Yr5
Revenue					
Placement fees	$312,500	$1,800,000	$5,184,000	$14,929,920	$32,248,627
Business sales	$ –	$2,750,000	$6,050,000	$13,310,000	$29,282,000
Business sales listing fee	$ –	$600,000	$990,000	$1,633,500	$2,695,275
Online training	$280,000	$1,108,800	$4,024,944	$14,610,547	$53,036,285
Books	$280,000	$616,000	$1,355,200	$2,981,440	$6,559,168
Employment opportunities	$252,000	$609,840	$1,475,813	$3,571,467	$8,642,950
Conferences	$ –	$1,320,000	$3,267,000	$8,085,825	$20,012,417
Service fees	$870,000	$1,914,000	$4,210,800	$9,263,760	$20,380,272
Sponsorship	$144,000	$316,800	$696,960	$1,533,312	$3,373,286
Total	$2,138,500	$11,035,440	$27,254,717	$69,919,771	$176,230,280

Years	Yr1	Yr2	Yr3	Yr4	Yr5
Expenses					
Salaries	$1,487,500	$3,233,250	$4,987,081	$8,179,149	$14,369,881
Taxes & benefits	$446,250	$969,975	$1,496,124	$2,453,745	$4,310,964
Travel	$331,429	$364,571	$401,029	$441,131	$485,245
Telephone	$49,714	$126,990	$204,696	$344,034	$607,112
Rent/utilities	$87,000	$222,233	$358,219	$602,059	$1,062,446
Marketing support	$215,000	$519,900	$695,010	$1,021,665	$1,667,259
Online training partner fees	$224,000	$887,040	$3,219,955	$11,688,437	$42,429,028
Book partner fees	$252,000	$554,400	$1,219,680	$2,683,296	$5,903,251
Business supplies	$16,571	$42,330	$68,232	$114,678	$202,371
Business technology	$49,714	$126,990	$204,696	$344,034	$607,112
Business sales	$ –	$2,612,500	$5,747,500	$12,644,500	$27,817,900
Conferences	$ –	$1,188,000	$2,940,300	$7,277,243	$18,011,175
Business equipment	$49,714	$126,990	$204,696	$344,034	$607,112
Technology	$376,000	$96,000	$125,100	$167,805	$230,870
Professional services	$220,000	$270,000	$333,000	$413,100	$515,970
Business insurance	$2,139	$11,035	$27,255	$69,920	$176,230
Miscellaneous	$76,141	$227,044	$444,651	$975,777	$2,380,079
Total expenses	$3,883,172	$11,579,248	$22,677,226	$49,764,607	$121,384,005
Pretax profit/loss	$(1,744,672)	$(543,808)	$4,577,491	$20,155,164	$54,846,275

Worldfunding.com

Minority member potential	25,000	30,000	36,000	43,200	51,840
Corporate potential	3,500	3,500	3,500	3,500	3,500
Revenue	Yr1	Yr2	Yr3	Yr4	Yr5
Member revenue	0	0	0	0	0
Minority vendors	0	0	0	0	0
No. of members	2,500	5,000	10,000	20,000	40,000
Price per membership	0	0	0	0	0
Corporate	0	0	0	0	0
No. of members	200	400	800	1,600	3,200

(continued)

Years	Yr1	Yr2	Yr3	Yr4	Yr5
Price per membership	0	0	0	0	0
Public/nonprofit	0	0	0	0	0
No. of members	100	200	400	800	1,600
Price per membership	0	0	0	0	0
Revenue					
Placement fees	$312,500	$1,800,000	$5,184,000	$14,929,920	$32,248,627
No. of deals	125	600	1,440	3,456	6,221
Average deal	$500,000	$600,000	$720,000	$864,000	$1,036,800
Referral fee (%)	0.005	0.005	0.005	0.005	0.005
Online training	$280,000	$1,108,800	$4,024,944	$14,610,547	$53,036,285
No. of corporate members	2,800	5,600	11,200	22,400	44,800
Percentage buying courses (%)	0.05	0.08	0.11	0.17	0.25
No. of courses	2.0	2.4	2.6	2.9	3.2
Charge per course	$1,000	$1,100	$1,210	$1,331	$1,464
Books	$280,000	$616,000	$1,355,200	$2,981,440	$6,559,168
No. of users	2,800	5,600	11,200	22,400	44,800
No. of books	4	4	4	4	4
Average price per book	$25	$28	$30	$33	$37
Employment opportunities	$252,000	$609,840	$1,475,813	$3,571,467	$8,642,950
No. of companies	140	280	560	1,120	2,240
Average number of ads	12	13	15	16	18
Cost per ad	$150	$165	$182	$200	$220
Business sales	$ –	$2,750,000	$6,050,000	$13,310,000	$29,282,000
No. of companies for sale	0	50	100	200	400
Average sale price	$500,000	$550,000	$605,000	$665,500	$732,050
Percentage sold (%)	0.10	0.10	0.10	0.10	0.10
Business sales listing fee	$ –	$600,000	$990,000	$1,633,500	$2,695,275
No. companies for sale	0	500	750	1,125	1,688

Years	Yr1	Yr2	Yr3	Yr4	Yr5
Charge per listing per year	0	$1,200	$1,320	$1,452	$1,597
Conferences	$ –	$1,320,000	$3,267,000	$8,085,825	$20,012,417
No. of conferences	0	4	6	9	14
Average number of attendees	200	300	450	675	1,013
Average attendance fee	$1,000	$1,100	$1,210	$1,331	$1,464
Service finder's fees	$870,000	$1,914,000	$4,210,800	$9,263,760	$20,380,272
No. of companies	2,500	5,000	10,000	20,000	40,000
No. of service providers	100	200	400	800	1,600
Membership fee	$1,200	$1,320	$1,452	$1,597	$1,757
Percentage of co's providing projects	0.10	0.10	0.10	0.10	0.10
Average project	$30,000	$33,000	$36,300	$39,930	$43,923
Minority vendors fee (%)	0.10	0.10	0.10	0.10	0.10
Sponsorships	$144,000	$316,800	$696,960	$1,533,312	$3,373,286
No. of sponsors	6	12	24	48	96
Average fee per month	$2,000	$2,200	$2,420	$2,662	$2,928
No. of months	12	12	12	12	12
Expenses					
Management salaries	$632,500	$959,500	$1,073,600	$1,202,922	$1,349,787
Chairman/CEO	1	1	1	1	1
Annual salary	$175,000	$192,500	$211,750	$232,925	$256,218
President/COO	1	1	1	1	1
Annual salary	$150,000	$165,000	$181,500	$199,650	$219,615
Vp of marketing	1	1	1	1	1
Annual salary	$62,500	$125,000	$137,500	$151,250	$166,375
VP of finance	0	1	1	1	1
Annual salary	$62,500	$125,000	$137,500	$151,250	$166,375
VP of sales	0	1	1	1	1
Annual salary	$62,500	$68,750	$75,625	$83,188	$91,506

(continued)

Years	Yr1	Yr2	Yr3	Yr4	Yr5
VP of content	1	1	1	1	1
Annual salary	$70,000	$77,000	$84,700	$93,170	$102,487
VP of banking relationships	1	1	1	1	1
Annual salary	$100,000	$110,000	$121,000	$133,100	$146,410
VP of technology	1	1	1	1	1
Annual salary	$75,000	$150,000	$165,000	$181,500	$199,650
Sales managers	$70,000	$147,000	$231,525	$567,236	$1,191,196
No. of managers	1	2	3	7	14
Annual salary	$70,000	$73,500	$77,175	$81,034	$85,085
Marketing directors	$55,000	$288,750	$303,188	$318,347	$334,264
No. of people	1	5	5	5	5
Annual salary	$55,000	$57,750	$60,638	$63,669	$66,853
Sales executives	$220,000	$693,000	$1,455,300	$3,056,130	$6,417,873
No. of people	4	12	24	48	96
Annual salary	$55,000	$57,750	$60,638	$63,669	$66,853
Content managers	$100,000	$157,500	$275,625	$405,169	$607,753
No. of people	2	3	5	7	10
Annual salary	$50,000	$52,500	$55,125	$57,881	$60,775
Customer service	$60,000	$94,500	$165,375	$243,101	$364,652
No. of CS reps	2	3	5	7	10
Annual salary	$30,000	$31,500	$33,075	$34,729	$36,465
Website personnel	$ –	$409,500	$716,625	$1,053,439	$1,422,142
Programmers	0	6	10	14	18
Annual salary	$65,000	$68,250	$71,663	$75,246	$79,008
Clerical assistance	1	2	2	3	5
Annual salary	$30,000	$31,500	$33,075	$34,729	$35,423
Total personnel	17	40	62	99	166
Taxes & benefits (% salary)	30%	30%	30%	30%	30%
Travel	$331,429	$364,571	$401,029	$441,131	$485,245
No. of employees	17	40	62	99	166

Years	Yr1	Yr2	Yr3	Yr4	Yr5
Average travel expense	$20,000	$21,000	$22,050	$23,153	$24,310
Telephone	$49,714	$126,990	$204,696	$344,034	$607,112
No. of employees	17	40	62	99	166
Telephone (per person)	$3,000	$3,150	$3,308	$3,473	$3,647
Rent/utilities	$87,000	$222,233	$358,219	$602,059	$1,062,446
No. of employees	17	40	62	99	166
Cost per sq. foot	$21	$22	$23	$24	$26
Sq. foot per person	250	250	250	250	250
Total marketing support	$215,000	$519,900	$695,010	$1,021,665	$1,667,259
Direct mail (postcards)	$37,000	$78,300	$165,750	$350,979	$743,445
No. of letters	100,000	200,000	400,000	800,000	1,600,000
Cost per mailing	$0.31	$0.33	$0.34	$0.36	$0.38
Cost per name	$0.06	$0.06	$0.06	$0.06	$0.06
Cost per post card	$1.00	$1.10	$1.21	$1.33	$1.46
Direct e-mail	$18,000	$39,600	$79,860	$167,706	$360,169
No. of mailings	6	12	12	12	12
Setup fee	$500	$550	$605	$666	$732
No. of lists	5	5	5	5	5
Cost per e-mail	$0.03	$0.03	$0.04	$0.04	$0.04
No. of mailings	100,000	200,000	400,000	800,000	1,600,000
Public relations	$60,000	$72,000	$86,400	$103,680	$124,416
No. of months	6	12	12	12	12
Fee per month	$10,000	$11,000	$12,100	$13,310	$14,641
Print advertising	$100,000	$330,000	$363,000	$399,300	$439,230
No. of ads	20	60	60	60	60
Cost per ad	$5,000	$5,500	$6,050	$6,655	$7,321
Sponsorships	$ –	$99,000	$145,200	$199,650	$263,538
No. of markets	0	6	8	10	12
Budget per market	$15,000	$16,500	$18,150	$19,965	$21,962

(continued)

Years	Yr1	Yr2	Yr3	Yr4	Yr5
Online training	$224,000	$887,040	$3,219,955	$11,688,437	$42,429,028
Revenue	$280,000	$1,108,800	$4,024,944	$14,610,547	$53,036,285
Fee to partner (%)	0.80	0.80	0.80	0.80	0.80
Books	$252,000	$554,400	$1,219,680	$2,683,296	$5,903,251
Revenue	$280,000	$616,000	$1,355,200	$2,981,440	$6,559,168
Fee to partner (%)	0.90	0.90	0.90	0.90	0.90
Business sales	$ –	$2,612,500	$5,747,500	$12,644,500	$27,817,900
Revenue	0	$2,750,000	$6,050,000	$13,310,000	$29,282,000
Fee to seller (%)	0.95	0.95	0.95	0.95	0.95
Conferences	$ –	$1,188,000	$2,940,300	$7,277,243	$18,011,175
Revenue	0	$1,320,000	$3,267,000	$8,085,825	$20,012,417
Fee to conferences (%)	0.90	0.90	0.90	0.90	0.90
Bus. supplies (pp per yr.)	$16,571	$42,330	$68,232	$114,678	$202,371
Employees	17	40	62	99	166
Cost for supplies	$1,000	$1,050	$1,103	$1,158	$1,216
Bus. equipment (pp per yr.)	$49,714	$126,990	$204,696	$344,034	$607,112
Employees	17	40	62	99	166
Cost of supplies	$3,000	$3,150	$3,308	$3,473	$3,647
Technology	$376,000	$96,000	$125,100	$167,805	$230,870
Website development/ maintenance	$300,000	$360,000	$432,000	$518,400	$622,080
Hosting	$36,000	$54,000	$81,000	$121,500	$182,250
SQL server & misc.	$5,000	$5,250	$5,513	$5,788	$6,078
Equipment	$35,000	$36,750	$38,588	$40,517	$42,543
Prof. srv. (legal, acct., HR)	$220,000	$270,000	$333,000	$413,100	$515,970
Legal	$50,000	$60,000	$72,000	$86,400	$103,680
Accounting	$20,000	$30,000	$45,000	$67,500	$101,250
Human resources	$50,000	$60,000	$72,000	$86,400	$103,680
IT	$100,000	$120,000	$144,000	$172,800	$207,360
Business insurance	$2,139	$11,035	$27,255	$69,920	$176,230
Miscellaneous	$76,141	$227,044	$444,651	$975,777	$2,380,079

Income

All income revenue is based on first year's experience and what management believes current and future partnerships will bring.

Investment capital: Based on percentages given by Eloan and Capital.com

Business sales: Based on what Sun Belt Business Owners charges

Online training: Based on what Phoenix, the top online education company, would pay a partner

Books: Based on what Amazon pays partners

Employment opportunities: Based on what Minorities Job Bank charges

Conferences: Based on figures provided by Association of Executive Directors

Service fees: Based on average rfpMarket's contract size

Sponsorship: Based on 1 cent per visitor per month

Expenses

Management salaries: Based on figures supplied by executive recruiting firms on what startup Internet companies are paying on average

Taxes and benefits: Based on a PricewaterhouseCoopers study on what companies pay on average to employees

Travel: Based on figures supplied by AAA

Telephone: Based on figures supplied by public relations department of Verizon

Telephone 800 service: Based on figures provided by AT&T small business services

Rent and utilities: Based on figures supplied by Building Owners and Managers Association

Direct mail: Based on figures provided by Direct Marketing Association

Magazine ads: Based on contacting and reviewing advertising press kits

Public relations: Based on contacting small and medium-sized public relations firms

Business supplies: Based on figures supplied by Staples public relations department

Business equipment: Based on figures supplied by Staples public relations department

Technology hosting: Based on speaking with Digger and Bee.Net

Professional services: Based on contacting professional service firms

Business insurance: Based on figures supplied by New England Financial

SAMPLE TERM SHEET

XYZ Technologies, Inc.
Term Sheet*

AC Management Services, Inc.

[Author's Note: XYZ Technologies is a company that was in a product development stage for about two years prior to approaching venture capitalists for financing. Up to this time, the company was wholly owned by the two founders who had put in personal financial resources and a full-time, noncompensated effort. The founders, in their own name, had developed and patented a sophisticated system that permitted on-site generation of a chemical that is used widely in a variety of industrial and medical settings. Installation and operation of these systems would provide significant economies for XYZ's customers. The patent position was very strong, the management credible, and the business strategy sound. On the basis of the company's status, a venture capital fund that managed several pools of capital, including funds from a state economic development organization, made an offer designed to capitalize the company and have it relocate to the venture fund's home state. The fund, ACT Partners, assisted in securing a factory site, at highly favorable terms, in a nearby city from the local government.

ACT also wanted to syndicate the deal with another local venture fund, ACORN, and a state agency, STATE. The facility was financed by the Council on Economic Development (CED).

---

*This term sheet was provided by Stephen M. Sammut, a biotech venture capitalist, and is used in the course that Mr. Sammut and the author teach in the MBA program at the Wharton School of Business of the University of Pennsylvania.

The venture capitalists were confident of XYZ's future, but did not want to have management's time occupied with future fund raising. Based on the company's operating plan, capital needs were forecasted to breakeven and positive cash flow. The total required investment would be committed, but would be made available to the company in a series of four "tranches." After months of negotiation, the following term sheet was accepted by both sides, and legal counsel directed to draft appropriate documents.]

Issuer

XYZ Technologies Corporation ("XYZ" or the "Company")

Securities

Convertible preferred stock (the "Preferred')

Offering Size

$3.5 million to be allocated among the investors as follows:

ACT:	$1.1 million
STATE:	$0.375 million
ACORN:	$2.025 million

Takedowns or tranches will be as follows:

$1.0 million at closing.

Prior to the initial closing, the Investors and management must have agreed on a final operating budget for the first 12 months, the use of proceeds for the initial takedown, and an allocation of the initial equity among management [nonfounders]. In addition, (a) all the intellectual property owned by the Founders (and/or related entities) that are (or potentially are) related to XYZ's business must have been transferred to XYZ, and (b) a "not to exceed" contract for the renovation of the Bridgeport facility should be in place.

$750,000 upon completion of a [Beta Test] unit to the satisfaction of the investors.

$1.0 million upon the satisfactory completion of the following milestones:

3.1	Sale of 250 units, including 150 to ABC Company;
3.2	Signing of one other North American distribution agreement which will project a minimum of $1 million of sales within 12 months of signing;
3.3	Hiring of a CFO acceptable to the Board.

$750,000 upon the satisfactory completion of the following milestones:

4.1	Cumulative revenues of $2.5 million;
4.2	Positive cash flow (net income + depreciation) in the aggregate for the previous three months of at least $500,000;
4.3	Five revenue-generating customers in place.

In addition, the Council on Economic Development (CED) will fund on a pro rata basis to the Preferred an aggregate of $3.5 million from a $1.75 million CED grant and a $1.75 million 10-year loan from CED whose terms and conditions will be satisfactory to the Investors (approximately a 10-year loan with a noncumulative interest rate of no more than 2%; interest payments deferred for at least 5 years). The loan will be entitled to security in the fixed assets (not including A/R0 of XYZ) and will have attached 5-year warrants to purchase a number of shares equal to 1% of the pro forma shares outstanding after the takedown of the Preferred.

Price

The pre-money value including all outstanding warrants and options, any authorized but unissued warrants and options (including a reasonable pool of a number of shares for future hires), all common and preferred shares, and any other outstanding equity equivalents will be $4.75 million. The pre-money value for the third closing will be 20% higher on a per share basis and the value for the fourth closing 20% higher than the per share closing on the third closing. In addition, the Investors will receive on a pro rata basis to each closing, warrants to purchase a number of preferred shares equal to 30% of the preferred shares so purchased at an exercise price equal to 125% of the preferred price per share. The exercise may be by cash or on a cashless basis at the sole option of the holder.

Use of Proceeds

The proceeds from the sale of the preferred stock will be used for working capital, sales expenditures, and further product research and development as more fully set forth in the Sources and Uses table to be approved by both the Company and Investors and appended to the financing document.

Dividends

Four percent (4%) per year, payable in stock or cash on a cumulative basis at the option of the Company beginning six (6) quarters after closing.

Redemption

The Preferred shall be redeemed at a cost in equal annual installments at the end of the years five to eight unless the stock shall have been previously converted into common stock.

Liquidation Rights

The holders of the Preferred will be entitled to a liquidation preference over the common stock. The liquidation preference will also apply in the event of a sale of all or substantially all the assets of the Company or a merger or consolidation of the Company. First, the Preferred will receive a return of capital. Any remaining proceeds shall be allocated between the common and preferred stockholders on a pro rata basis, treating the Preferred on an as-if-converted basis.

Optional Conversion

At any time at the holder's option, the Preferred may be converted into common stock on a one-for-one basis or at such rates as result from the application of antidilution (see below).

Mandatory Conversion

The Preferred will be converted at the Company's option concurrently with the closing of the initial public offering of the Company's common stock so long as the aggregate amount raised by such offering equals or exceeds a common share price of at least three times the conversion price of the Preferred.

Voting Rights

The Preferred will have full voting rights equal to the number of shares of common stock into which the Preferred may be converted. A vote of 51% of the Preferred (such vote not to be unreasonably withheld) will be required for the Company to engage in an extraordinary act including (exceptions to be decided by the Board will be so noted):

Adoption of the annual budget by the Board of Directors by less than a two-thirds affirmative vote;

Incurring third-party indebtedness above $250,000 in any one year will be subject to Board approval;

Incurring any capital expenditure above $250,000 in any one year will be subject to Board approval;

Sale of any material asset or the sale, merger, or consolidation of the Company into or with any other entity;

Purchase or redemption of any Company securities or any cash distributions to equity holders (other than the repurchase of shares of terminating employees);

Issuance or sale of Company securities with rights, preferences, and privileges senior to or on parity with the Preferred;

Changing the nature of the business in any material way or any material change to the Company's Business Plan;

Transactions with affiliates except as approved by the Board of Directors by a two-thirds or greater affirmative vote;

The amendment of the Company's articles of incorporation or bylaws that adversely affects the preferred shareholders or any rights, preferences, or privileges granted to Investors therein or herein;

A change in the number of authorized directors;

A liquidation or dissolution of the Company, or a reclassification of its outstanding capital stock.

Antidilution Adjustments

Conversion ratio adjusted on a standard weighted average basis. "Dilutive issuance" shall not include common stock issued or issuable to employees, directors, and consultants pursuant to the option plan currently in existence or any other plan or amendment approved by holders of 50% of the Preferred.

Proportional adjustments for stock splits and stock dividends will not trigger antidilution adjustments.

NOTE: To accommodate this provision, legal counsel essentially had to create a separate series of preferred stock for each takedown or tranche because of the different prices negotiated for shares that would be issued in each tranche.

Board

The Preferred holders will be entitled to elect two (2) Board positions out of a five-person Board. AIPLP and ACORN are each entitled to designate one member. For serving on the Board, the Venture representatives will receive options to purchase 1,000 shares of Preferred (at the initial purchase price per share) for each meeting attended. The other Board members will include the Founder (assuming the Founder owns greater than 20% of the Company), a management representative, and a mutually acceptable outsider. If the Founder owns less than 20%, the seat will be represented by management.

Nondisclosure and Proprietary Information Agreement

The founders and key employees of the Company will enter into Nondisclosure and Proprietary Information Agreements with the Company in form reasonably acceptable to the Company and the investors.

Vesting of Common Stock

Management common stock (including founder's stock) and options to buy common stock will vest over a five-year period. Founder's founders' stock will be 40% vested on the day of closing. The remaining stock (60%) will vest over five years. In the event of voluntary or "with cause" involuntary termination, unvested stock will be forfeited to the Company. *With cause* refers to behavior or actions that are illegal, immoral, etc., and that a continuing association as management of the Company will have a detrimental influence on the Company. The continued vesting of founder stock for Founder will be based on Company's performance relative to the final approved budget at closing. Vesting will proceed as defined above as long as the Company achieves 80% of its operating income budget, and if the Company sells X number of systems by month 10 after closing with at least half sold in the USA.

In the event that the Company does not achieve 80% of its operating budget in any six-month period, there will be six months to remedy the cumulative shortfall. If the cumulative shortfall is not remedied to be 80% of operating income budget after this period, the Board has the authority to remove Founder as CEO, and terminate his employment by a majority vote of the Board of Directors.

Each holder of the Preferred will be furnished by the Company with an annual budget and annual audited financial statements within 90 days following the end of each fiscal year as well as monthly financials. In addition, the Company must deliver an operating plan no later than 60 days prior to the end of each fiscal year.

Shareholders Agreement

A Shareholders Agreement will be entered into among significant equity holders of the Company's common stock. Such agreement shall include, among others, the following Provision:

Transfer of Interests: No party may sell, transfer, or otherwise dispose of any equity interest (except in case of the sale of the entire Company as approved by the Company's Board and the holders of a majority of Preferred) other than as permitted in the Shareholders Agreement.

Right of First Refusal

Investors shall be afforded a right of first refusal to participate in any sale of company securities upon the same terms and conditions as proposed by the Company. The participation rights will be in proportion to the investors' ownership position prior to the offering. In the event of such proposed sale and issuance, Investors shall be given a 30-day notice and period in which to act upon such proposal.

Tag Along

Investors shall be afforded a "tag-along" right that will provide that in the event the Company or the Company's shareholders receive a solicited or unsolicited proposal from a third party to acquire all or some of their equity securities, the offeree(s) shall be required to make such proposal available to all the Company's equity holders on a pro rata basis.

Registration Rights Agreement

Investors and the Company shall enter into a Registration Rights Agreement providing for the registration of shares of common stock issued upon conversion of the Preferred upon the following terms:

Company Registration: The investors shall be entitled to "piggyback" registration rights on all registrations of the Company subject to the right, however, of the Company and its underwriters in good faith to reduce the number of shares proposed to be registered pro rata among all investors in view of market conditions.

S-3 Rights: Investors shall be entitled to two (2) demand registrations on Form S-3 (if available to the Company) so long as such registered offerings are not less than $500,000.

Expenses: The Company shall bear registration expenses (exclusive of underwriting discounts and commissions) of all such piggybacks and S-3 registrations (including the expense of a single counsel to the selling shareholders not to exceed $10,000).

Standoff Provisions: If requested by the underwriters, no investor or any other shareholder will sell shares of the Company's stock for up to 180 days following a public offering by the Company of its stock.

Termination of Rights: The registration rights shall terminate on the date three years after the Company's initial public offering, or with respect to each investor, at such time as (1) the Company's shares are publicly traded and (2) the investor is entitled to sell all of its shares in any 90-day period pursuant to Securities Act Rule 144.

Directors' and Officers' Indemnification

The Company will represent that it has provisions in its articles or bylaws for the indemnification of officers and directors to the full extent permitted by law and will covenant to keep such indemnification in place for so long as any representative of the Investors serves on the Board of Directors.

Directors' and Officers' Liability Insurance

The Company will use its best efforts to obtain and keep directors' and officers' liability insurance in the minimum amount of $1,000,000 if such coverage is available at commercially acceptable rates.

Other

The company will obtain key man insurance in the amount of $2 million. All applicable issued patents, patent applications, patent applications in progress, and any future inventions associated with the Company, in any jurisdiction, shall be assigned to the Company, regardless of field of use.

Prior to the initial closing, the Company will have entered into employment agreements with: [key management] acceptable to Investors.

There will be reimbursement to the investors of (a) legal expenses up to a maximum of $25,000 for preparing the documents associated with the financing and (b) consultants' fees incurred in connection with "due diligence" up to a maximum of $5,000.

Representations and Warranties

Standard representations and warranties.

Signatures

The undersigned acknowledge that this term sheet represents a nonbinding agreement in principle. All parties maintain the right to withdraw any offer herein contained, or further negotiate terms and conditions.

_____	_____	_____	_____
XYZ Founders	Date	XYZ Founders	Date
_____	_____	_____	_____
ACT	Date	ACORN	Date
_____	_____	_____	_____
STATE	Date	CED	Date

SAMPLE PRIVATE PLACEMENT
MEMORANDUM

ABC HOLDINGS, INC.
Series B Convertible Preferred Stock
Summary of Preliminary Proposed Terms

I. The Offering

Issuer:	ABC Holdings, Inc. (the "Company").
Issue:	Private Placement of Series B Convertible Preferred Stock (the "Series B Preferred Stock") offered to accredited investors only pursuant to Regulation D.
Amount:	Minimum of $2.5 million and maximum of $7.5 million, exclusive of an overallotment option of up to $2.5 million to be issued by the Company (the "Greenshoe").
Pre-Offering Valuation (Fully Diluted):	$7.0 million
Use of Proceeds:	Acquisitions
Purchase Agreement:	The Series B Preferred Stock shall be purchased pursuant to a Stock Purchase Agreement that shall contain representations, warranties, and covenants of the Company and conditions to closing customary for a transaction of this kind.
Estimated Closing Date:	Within three months from the date of the Placement Agent Agreement.

II. Summary of Preferred Stock Terms

Right of Conversion:	Each share of Series B Preferred Stock is convertible at any time (at the option of the holder) initially on a share-for-share basis into the Company's Common Stock (the "Common Stock").
Automatic Conversion:	Each share of Series B Preferred Stock shall automatically be converted into shares of Common Stock at the closing of an initial public offering in which the gross proceeds to the Company are not less than $10 million and the investors of the Series B Preferred Stock realize an annual average rate of return of 40% (a "Qualified Public Offering").
Dividend Provisions:	The holders of the Series B Preferred Stock shall be entitled to receive cumulative dividends at the rate of 8% per annum when, as, and if declared by the Board of Directors.
Seniority:	Any future issue of preferred stock shall not be senior to the Series B Preferred Stock, except upon the consent of at least 67% of the then outstanding shares of the Series B Preferred Stock.
Liquidation Preference:	The holders of the Series B Preferred Stock shall be entitled to receive prior and in preference to any distribution of any of the assets of the Company or proceeds thereof to the holders of Common Stock (the "Liquidation Preference").
Merger, Consolidation, or Sale:	Upon the consolidation or merger of the Company in which stockholders of the Company own less than 50% of the voting securities of the resulting or surviving corporation, or the sale or transfer of all or substantially all the assets of the Company, the holders of the Series B Preferred Stock shall have the option to (i) receive the Liquidation Preference plus accrued and unpaid dividends or (ii) participate with the holders of Common Stock on an as-converted basis.
Voting Rights:	The holders of Series B Preferred Stock shall be entitled to vote with the Common Stock of the Company as a single class on the basis of one vote per share of Series B Preferred Stock.

Registration Rights:	The holders of the Series B Preferred Stock will be entitled to certain demand and piggyback registration rights for the Common Stock to be received upon conversion of the Series B Preferred Stock following an initial public offering.
Mandatory Redemption:	On or after the earlier of (i) five years from the date of the closing hereunder or (ii) the date at which any other series of preferred stock is entitled to mandatory redemption, the holders of the Series B Preferred Stock shall have the option of "putting" their Series B Preferred Stock back to the Company for the Liquidation Preference plus any accrued and unpaid dividends.
Antidilution Provisions:	The holders of the Series B Preferred Stock shall have certain antidilution provisions that shall be calculated on a weighted average basis.
Preemptive Right (Right of First Refusal):	Holders of the Series B Preferred Stock shall have the same right of first refusal providing for the purchase of shares of future private offerings of equity securities (or warrants or other securities convertible into equity securities) of the Company that will enable them to maintain their fully-diluted percentage ownership of the Company. This right shall terminate upon a Qualified Public Offering.
Tag-Along Provision (Co-sale rights):	In the event that an offer is made to purchase shares of Common Stock owned by any officers, directors, or 5% holders of the Company, the holders of the Series B Preferred Stock shall have the right to sell a pro rata portion of their shares to such purchaser.
Board of Directors:	The holders of the Series B Preferred Stock, as a class, will be entitled to designate one (1) member of the Board of Directors which shall consist of no more than five (5) members of which three (3) shall be outsiders.
Information Rights and Access:	The holders of the Series B Preferred Stock and Darren Keith & Company, Inc., shall have the right to promptly receive: (i) quarterly unaudited financial statements within 45 days after the end

of each quarter; (ii) annual audited financial statements within 90 days after the end of each year; (iii) a budget and operating plan for each year at least 45 days prior to the start of each year; (iv) copies of all reports sent to stockholders or filed with the SEC; (v) notification of material litigation; and (vi) other information as reasonably requested.

Amendments and Waivers of Rights:	Amendments to and waivers of the rights of the holders of the Series B Preferred Stock must be approved by the holders of 67% of the Series B Preferred Stock.

III. Placement Agent Compensation

Exclusive Placement Agent:	Darren Keith & Company, Inc.
Placement Agent Fee:	Eight percent (8%) of the total amount raised. The Company shall receive a credit of three percent (3%) for any amount raised from officers, directors, and predetermined friends of the Company.
Expense Allowance:	Fifty thousand dollars ($50,000), twenty-five thousand ($25,000) of which is payable upon the signing of a Placement Agent Agreement.
Warrants:	Five-year warrants to purchase common stock equal to 10% of the number of as-converted shares of the Series B Preferred Stock sold hereunder at a 10% premium to the conversion price.
Other:	Upon closing of the Offering, Darren Keith & Company, Inc., shall have a right of first refusal for all investment banking activities of the Company for a period of two years from the final closing of this Offering and shall have observer rights to meetings of the Board of Directors until the Company's initial public offering. The Darren Keith & Company, Inc., observer shall be promptly reimbursed for reasonable out-of-pocket expenses incurred in attending such meetings.

APPENDIX D

INVESTOR GROUPS AND FUNDS

PRIVATE INVESTOR AND VENTURE GROUPS

ALABAMA

Birmingham Venture Club
c/o Birmingham Chamber of
  Commerce
P.O. Box 10127
Birmingham, AL 35202
205-323-5461

Hickory Venture Group
301 Washington St., NW, Suite 301
Huntsville, AL 35801
256-539-1931
www.hvcc.com

ALASKA

Alaska InvestNet
Juneau Economic Development
  Council
612 W. Willoughby, Suite A
Juneau, AK 99801
907-463-3662
www.ptialaska.net/-jedc

Alaska Pacific Venture Club
405 W. 27th Ave.
Anchorage, AK 99503
907-563-3993

ARIZONA

Arizona Technology Venture Fund
1435 N. Hayden Rd.
Scottsdale, AZ 85257-3773
480-990-0400
www.accessarizona.com

Arizona Ventures
2419 N. Black Canyon Highway
Suite 4
Phoenix, AZ 85009
602-254-8560

Enterprise Network
7225 W. Oakland St.
Chandler, AZ 85226
480-496-4408
www.en.org

ARKANSAS

Venture Capital Investors, Inc.
2323 First Commercial Building
400 W. Capitol Ave.
Little Rock, AR 72201-3441
501-372-8181

Venture Resources, Inc.
100 S. Main St., Suite 416
Little Rock, AR 72201
501-375-2004

CALIFORNIA

Bay Area Venture Forum
International Capital Resources
388 Market St., Suite 500
San Francisco, CA 94111
415-296-2519
www.icrnet.com

Greenhouse Venture Group
977 Shotwell St., Suite 100
San Francisco, CA 94110
415-401-0577
Greenhousefourstartups.com

Investors Circle
1 Coleridge St., Suite B
San Francisco, CA 94110
415-641-0204
www.investorscircle.net

Los Angeles Venture Association
1247 Lincoln Blvd., #129
Santa Monica, CA 90401
Phone 310-450-9544
Fax 310-395-0657
www.lava.org

Northern California Venture Forum
388 Market St., Suite 500
San Francisco, CA 94111
415-296-2519
www.icrnet.com

Orange Coast Venture Group
23011 Moulton Parkway, Suite F-2
Laguna Hills, CA 92653
949-859-3646
www.ocv.org

Sacramento Area Venture Capital
  Network
Addexton Co.
P.O. Box 73585
Davis, CA 95617-3585
530-753-3753
www.sacareavcnetwork.com

San Diego Venture Group
750 B St., Suite 2400
San Diego, CA 92101
619-595-0284

COLORADO

Colorado Capital Alliance, Inc.
P.O. Box 19169
Boulder, CO 80020
303-404-8818
www.angelcapital.org

Rockies Venture Club
190 E. 9th Ave., Suite 440
Denver, CO 80203
303-831-4174
www.rockiesventureclub.org

CONNECTICUT

Connecticut Venture Group
425 Katona Dr.
Fairfield, CT 06430
203-333-3284

DELAWARE

Delaware Entrepreneurs Forum
P.O. Box 278
Yorklyn, DE 19736
302-652-4241

FLORIDA

Central Florida Innovation Corp.
12424 Research Parkway, Suite 350
Orlando, FL 32826
407-277-0544
www.cfic.org

Florida Venture Forum
Florida International University
2600 Douglas Rd., Suite 311
Coral Gables, FL 33134
305-446-5060

Gold Coast Venture Capital Club
1140-A W. Palmetto Park Rd.
Suite 202
Boca Raton, FL 33428
561-488-4505

GEORGIA

Atlanta Development Authority
230 Peachtree St., N.W., Suite 2100
Atlanta, GA 30303
404-658-7000

Atlanta Venture Forum, Inc.
One Atlantic Center
1201 W. Peachtree St.
Atlanta, GA 30339-3450
404-873-8522

HAWAII

Hawaii Venture Capital Association
805 Kainui Dr.
Kailua, HI 96734-2025
808-262-7329

IDAHO

Rocky Mountain Venture Group
2300 No. Yellowstone
Idaho Falls, ID 83401
208-526-1181

INDIANA

Indiana Private Investor's Network
216 W. Allen St.
Bloomington, IN 47403
812-339-8937

Michiana Investment Network
300 N. Michigan
South Bend, IN 46601
219-282-4350

Private Investors Network
216 W. Allen St.
Bloomington, IN 47403
812-339-8937

Venture Club of Indiana
P.O. Box 40872
Indianapolis, IN 46240
317-253-1244
www.ventureclub.org

IOWA

Venture Network of Iowa
Greater Des Moines Chamber of
  Commerce
200 East Grand Ave.
Des Moines, IA 50309
800-532-1216
www.state.ia.us

KENTUCKY

Venture Club of Louisville
304 W. Liberty, Suite 301
Louisville, KY 40202
502-589-6868
www.ventureclub-louisville.org

LOUISIANA

The Venture Network
P.O. Box 30240
New Orleans, LA 70190
504-527-6936

MAINE

Maine Investment Exchange
Maine Chamber and Business Alliance
120 Exchange St.
Portland, ME 04101
207-774-1001
www.maineco.org

MARYLAND

Baltimore–Washington Venture Group
Dingman Center for Entrepreneurship
Maryland Business School
The University of Maryland
College Park, MD 20742-1815
301-405-2144
www.mbs.umd.edu\dingman

Private Investors Network
7201 Wisconsin Ave., Suite 210
Bethesda, MD 20814
301-718-4272
www.newvantagepartners.com

MASSACHUSETTS

Technology Capital Network, Inc.
290 Main St.
Bldg. E-39, Lower Level
Cambridge, MA 02142
617-253-7163

Venture-Preneurs Network
85 E. India Row, Suite 23B
Boston, MA 02110
617-720-1535
www.tiac.net/users/vpn

MICHIGAN

Jackson Venture Capital Forum
Jackson Business Development Center
414 No. Jackson St.
Jackson, MI 49201
517-787-0442

Southeastern Michigan Venture Club
20630 Harper Ave., Suite 103
Harper Woods, MI 48225
313-886-2331

Traverse Bay Enterprise Forum
P.O. Box 506
Traverse City, MI 49685-0506
616-929-5017

MINNESOTA

Minnesota Investment Network
  Corporation
1600 University Ave., W., Suite 401
St. Paul, MN 55104
651-632-2140

New Venture Collaborative
10 S. Fifth St., Suite 415
Minneapolis, MN 55402-1004
612-338-3828
www.collaborative-online.com

MISSOURI

Missouri Venture Forum
1173 N. Price Rd.
St Louis, MO 63132
314-241-2683
www.ventureforum.org

NEW JERSEY

Venture Association of New Jersey
P.O. Box 1982
Morristown, NJ 07962-1982
973-631-5680

NEW YORK

Long Island Venture Group
Roth Hall, Room 309
Long Island University, C.W. Post
  Campus
Northern Blvd.
Brookville, NY 11548
516-299-3017

Silicon Alley Breakfast Club
TECHmarketing
91 Highland Rd.
Scarsdale, NY 10583
800-273-2832
www.Ibreakfast.com

The New York Angel Investors
  Program
New York New Media Association
55 Broad St.
New York, NY 10004
212-785-7898
www.nynma.org

Western New York Venture
  Association
Baird Research Park
1576 Sweet Home Rd.
Amherst, NY 14228
716-636-3626

NORTH CAROLINA

North Carolina Venture Capital
  Association
2700 Coltsgate Rd., Suite 202
Charlotte, NC 28211
704-362-3909

OHIO

Greater Cincinnati Venture
  Association
441 Vine St.
300 Carew Tower
Cincinnati, OH 45202-2812
513-686-2946
www2.xec.com/gcva

Miami Valley Venture Association
137 N. Main St., Suite 702
Dayton, OH 45402-1729
937-228-1141
www.mvva.org

Ohio Venture Association
1127 Euclid Ave., Suite 343
Cleveland, OH 44115
216-566-8884
www.ohioventure.org

OKLAHOMA

Oklahoma Investment Forum
616 S. Boston, Suite 100
Tulsa, OK 74119-1298
918-585-1201

OREGON

Oregon Entrepreneurs Forum
Portland, OR
503-222-2270

PENNSYLVANIA

Greater Philadelphia Venture Group
200 S. Broad St., Suite 700
Philadelphia, PA 19102-3896
215-790-3689
www.gpvg.com

Loosely Organized Retired Executives
  (LORE)
c/o Verus Corporation
5 Radnor Corporate Center
100 Matsonford Rd., Suite 105
Radnor, PA 19087
610-964-8452

Pennsylvania Private Investors Group
610 York Rd., Suite 107
Jenkintown, PA 19046
215-884-9300 (x140)
www.ppig.com

RHODE ISLAND

Brown University Venture Forum
P.O. Box 1949
Providence, RI 02912
401-863-3528
www.bdcri.com

SOUTH CAROLINA
Dare to Deal–Southeast Capital
 Connection
Center for Entrepreneurship,
 College of Charleston
310 Meeting St.
Charleston, SC 29424-0001
803-953-5628

SOUTH DAKOTA
Dakota Ventures
P.O. Box 8194
Rapid City, SD 57709
605-348-8441

TEXAS
Capital Network, Inc. (TCN)
3925 W. Braker Lane, Suite 406
Austin, TX 78759-5321
512-305-0826
www.thecapitalnetwork.com

UTAH
Mountain West Venture Group
Wayne Brown Institute
P.O. Box 2135
Salt Lake City UT 84110
801-595-1141
www.mwvg.org

VERMONT
Vermont Investor's Forum
c/o Green Mountain Capital
RD 1, Box 1503
Waterbury, VT 05676
802-244-8981

VIRGINIA
Charlottesville Venture Group
P.O. Box 1474
Charlottesville, VA 22902
804-979-7259
www.cville-venture.org

Hampton Roads Private Investor
 Network
Small Business Development Center
 of Hampton Roads
400 Bank St.
Norfolk, VA 23501
757-825-2957
www.hrccva.com

Richmond Venture Capital Club
1407 Huguenot Rd.
Midlothian, VA 23113
804-794-1117

WASHINGTON
Northwest Venture Group
P.O. Box 21693
Seattle, WA 98111
425-746-1973
www.nwvg.org

WISCONSIN
Wisconsin Venture Network
P.O. Box 92093
Milwaukee, WI 53202
414-224-7070
richard_b_bennett@em.fcnbd.com

CANADA—ONTARIO
MIT Enterprise Forum
Toronto, CN
416-736-5708

RUSSIA
DIC Investment Club
St. Petersburg, Russia
001-7-812-230-8884
investor@spb.cityline.ru

ASSOCIATIONS AND SOURCES

NATIONAL TRADE ASSOCIATIONS

Association of Small Business Development Centers
1050 17th St., N.W., #810
Washington, DC 20036
202-887-5599

International Venture Capital Institute
Box 1333
Stamford, CT 06904
203-323-3143

National Association of Seed and Venture Funds
301 N.W. 63rd St., Suite 500
Oklahoma City, OK 73116
405-843-6550
www.nasvf.org

National Association of Small Business Investment Companies
1156 15th St., #1101
Washington, DC 20005

Nation Venture Capital Association
1655 N. Fort Meyer Dr., #700
Arlington, VA 22209
703-351-5269
www.nvca.org

Western Association of Venture Capitalists
3000 Sand Hill Rd., Building 1, #90
Menlo Park, CA 94025
412-854-1322

INFORMATION SOURCES

American Venture Magazine
621 S.W. Alder, Suite 630
Portland, OR 97205
503-221-9981

DataMerge, Inc.
4521 E. Virginia Ave., Suite 201
Denver, CO 80222
303-320-8361
www.datamerge.com

Pratt's Guide to Venture Capital
Venture Economics, Inc.
40 W. 57th St., Suite 802
New York, NY 10019
212-765-5311

Vencap Data Quest
AI Research Corp.
2003 St. Julien Court
Mountain View, CA 94043-5411
415-852-9140

ANGEL WEBSITES

- American Business Funding Directory, *www.businessfinance.com*
- British Venture Capital Association, *www.brainstorm.co.uk/BVCA*
- Business Angels, *www.businessangels.com.au*
- Capital.com, *www.capital.com*
- Capital Match, *www.capmatch.com*
- Capital Matchmaker, *www.matchmaker.org*
- DMOZ, *www.dmoz.org/Business/Venture_Capital*
- Garage, *www.garage.com*
- LiveInvestors Forum, *www.liveinvestorsforum.com*
- OffRoad Capital Corporation, *www.offroadcapital.com*
- Robin Hood Ventures, *www.robinhood.com*
- Tri-State Private Investors Group, *www.angelinvestorfunding.com*
- Vcapital.com, *www.vcapital.com*
- Venture Associates, *www.venturea.com/clubs2.htm*
- Venture Highway, *www.venturehighway.com*
- Womenangels.net, *www.womenangels.net*

VENTURE CAPITAL EARLY-STAGE WEBSITES

- Axxon Capital, *www.axxoncapital.com*
- Battery Ventures, *www.battery.com*

- Benchmark Capital, *www.benchmark.com*
- Boston Millennia Partners, *www.millenniapartners.com*
- Boulder Ventures, *www.boulderventures.com*
- Capital Across America, *www.capitalacrossamerica.org*
- CMGI, *www.cmgi.com*
- Comcast Interactive Capital Group, *www.Comcast.com*
- Constellation Ventures, *www.constellationventures.com*
- Crosspoint Ventures Partners, *www.cpvp.com*
- Divine Interventures, *www.divineinterventures.com*
- Draper Fisher, *www.draper.com*
- Euclid Partners, *www.Euclidpartners.com*
- Flatiron, *www.flatironpartners.com*
- GeoCapital Partners, *www.geocapital.com*
- Grand Central Holdings, *www.grandcentralholdings.com*
- Grotech Capital Group, *www.grotech.com*
- Hudson Venture Partners, *www.hudsonptr.com*
- Hummer Winbald Venture Partners, *www.humwin.com*
- Idealabs, *www.idealabs.com*
- Internet Capital Group, *www.internetcapital.com*
- JK&B Capital, *www.jkbcapital.com*
- Keystone Venture Fund, *www.keystonevc.com*
- Kleiner Perkins Caufield, *www.kpc.com*
- Liberty Advisors, *www.libertyvc.com*
- Lycos Ventures, *www.lycosventures.com*
- Mellon Ventures, *www.mellonventures.com*
- MidAtlantic Venture Fund, *www.mavf.com*
- New Enterprise Associates, *www.nea.com*
- North Atlantic Technology Fund, *www.natf.com*
- Novak Biddle Venture Partners, *www.novakbiddle.com*
- Odin Capital Group, *www.odincapital.com*
- Olympic Venture Partners, *www.ovp.com*
- Pa Early Stage Venture Fund, *www.paearlystage.com*
- Prospect Street Ventures, *www.prospectventures.com*
- RAF NetVentures, *www.rafventures.com*

- RRE Ventures, *www.rre.com*
- Safeguard Scientifics, *www.safeguard.com*
- Sentinel Capital Partners, *www.sentinelpartners.com*
- SGI Capital, *www.sgicapital.com*
- Softbank, *www.softbank.com*
- Summit Partners, *www.summitpartners.com*
- Sutter Hill Ventures, *www.shv.com*
- Technology Leaders, *www.tlventures.com*
- Technology Partners, *www.edelsontech.com*
- Toucan Capital Corporation, *www.toucancapital.com*
- Venrock, *www.venrock.com*
- Viridian Capital, *www.viridiancapital.com*
- Women's Growth Capital Fund, *www.wgcf.com*

Index

A

accountants
    on boards of directors, 99
    company valuation and, 158
    consultant, evaluating, 82–86
    locating management candidates
        through, 74
    as service providers, 91
    venture capitalists requirements
        and, 140
advisory boards, 93–94
    establishing, 7
    listed in operating plan, 24
    sample operating plan for, 35
    selecting/evaluating members,
        94–98
antidilution adjustments, term sheets
    requirements for, 216
arrogance, in management teams, 56
associates, past, selecting management
    teams and, 58
Association of Association Executive
    Directors, 5
attorneys
    on boards of directors, 99
    company valuation and, 158
    importance of, 87–91
    investment deal role of, 150–51
    locating management candidates
        through, 74
    as service providers, 91
    special knowledge of, 151

venture capitalists requirements
    and, 140
authority, motivating employees with,
    76
automotive businesses, regional online
    opportunities, 2

B

bank financing, 117–19
bankers, as service providers, 91
barriers to entry, 18
Bell, Vincent G., Jr., on private
    investors' expectations, 130–33
board of advisors. *See* advisory boards
board of directors, 93
    building/using, 98–101
    members investments, 132
    optical to investment deals and,
        153–54
    selecting/evaluating members,
        94–98
    term sheets requirements for, 216
    venture capitalist requirements and,
        140
boarding schools, online opportunities
    for, 4
brokerage houses, identifying markets
    with, 5
business contracts, borrowing against,
    118